A History of Suction-Type Laminar-Flow Control with Empahsis on Flight Research

by
Albert L. Braslow

NASA History Division
Office of Policy and Plans
NASA Headquarters
Washington, DC 20546

Monographs in
Aerospace History
Number 13
1999

Table of Contents

Foreword

Laminar-flow control is an area of aeronautical research that has a long history at NASA's Langley Research Center, Dryden Flight Research Center, their predecessor organizations, and elsewhere. In this monograph, Albert L. Braslow, who spent much of his career at Langley working with this research, presents a history of that portion of laminar-flow technology known as active laminar-flow control, which employs suction of a small quantity of air through airplane surfaces. This important technique offers the potential for significant reduction in drag and, thereby, for large increases in range or reductions in fuel usage for aircraft. For transport aircraft, the reductions in fuel consumed as a result of laminar-flow control may equal 30 percent of present consumption.

Given such potential, it is obvious that active laminar-flow control with suction is an important technology. In this study, Al covers the early history of the subject and brings the story all the way to the mid-1990s with an emphasis on flight research, much of which has occurred here at Dryden. This is an important monograph that not only encapsulates a lot of history in a brief compass but also does so in language that is accessible to non-technical readers. NASA is publishing it in a format that will enable it to reach the wide audience the subject deserves.

Kevin L. Petersen
Director, Dryden Flight Research Center
February 18, 1999

Preface

This monograph is the result of a contract with the NASA Dryden History Office to write a brief history of laminar-flow-control research with an emphasis on flight research, especially that done at what is today the Dryden Flight Research Center (DFRC). I approached the writing of this history from the perspective of an engineer who had spent much of his career working on laminar-flow-control research and writing about the results in technical publications. I found out that writing history is quite a bit different from technical writing, but I hope that what I have written will explain laminar-flow control to the non-technical reader while at the same time providing historical background to the interested technical reader.

After completion of the final draft of this technical history in October 1998, I was made aware of NASA TP-1998-208705, October 1998, by Ronald D. Joslin, entitled *Overview of Laminar Flow Control*. Although some overlap exists between this publication and my own, as would be expected from the two titles, Joslin's intent was quite different from mine. He provides an extensive technical summary for engineers, scientists and technical managers of the content of many key papers without much evaluation of the significance of specific results over the years.

I would like to express my gratitude to the following DFRC personnel: David Fisher, Lisa Bjarke, and Daniel Banks for reading the initial draft; Jim Zeitz for reworking the figures; and Stephen Lighthill for doing the layout. My special thanks go to J.D. (Dill) Hunley, DFRC historian, who patiently guided this technical author through the vagaries of historical composition.

Albert L. Braslow
Newport News, Virginia
19 February 1999

A History of Suction-Type Laminar-Flow Control

Laminar-Flow Control Concepts and Scope of Monograph

This monograph presents a history of suction-type laminar-flow-control research in the National Advisory Committee for Aeronautics and its successor organization, the National Aeronautics and Space Administration, plus selected other organizations, with an emphasis on flight research. Laminar-flow control is a technology that offers the potential for improvements in aircraft fuel usage, range or endurance that far exceed any known single aeronautical technology. For transport-type airplanes, e.g., the fuel burned might be decreased a phenomenal 30 percent. Fuel reduction will not only help conserve the earth's limited supply of petroleum but will also reduce engine emissions and, therefore, air pollution. In addition, lower fuel usage will reduce the operating costs of commercial airplanes at least eight percent, depending upon the cost of the fuel and, therefore, will curtail ticket prices for air travel. Laminar-flow control is also the only aeronautical technology that offers the capability of designing a transport airplane that can fly nonstop without refueling from anywhere in the world to anywhere else in the world or that can remain aloft without refueling for approximately 24 hours. These enormous performance improvements that are potentially available for commercial or military applications, therefore, have made the concept the "pot of gold at the end of the rainbow" for aeronautical researchers.

A brief review of some of the fundamentals involved will improve an understanding of this technological history. When a solid surface moves through a fluid (such as the air), frictional forces drag along a thin layer of the fluid adjacent to the surface due to the viscosity (stickiness) of the fluid. A distinguished theoretician, Ludwig Prandtl, showed in 1904 how the flow around a solid body can be divided into two regions for analysis—this thin layer of fluid adjacent to the surface, called the boundary layer, where fluid friction plays an essential part, and the remaining region outside the boundary layer where friction may be neglected. The boundary layer generally exists in one of two states: laminar, where fluid elements remain in well-ordered nonintersecting layers (laminae), and turbulent, where fluid elements totally mix. The frictional force between the fluid and the surface, known as viscous drag, is much larger in a turbulent boundary layer than in a laminar one because of momentum losses associated with the mixing action. The energy required to overcome this frictional force on an airplane is a substantial part of the total energy required to move the airplane through the air. In the case of a transport airplane flying at subsonic speeds, for example, approximately *one-half* of the energy (fuel) required to maintain level flight in cruise results from the necessity to overcome the skin friction of the boundary layer, which is mostly turbulent on current transport-size airplanes.

The state of the boundary layer, in the absence of disturbing influences, is directly related to the speed of the surface and the distance along the surface—first, laminar and then changing to turbulent as the speed or distance increases. Laminar flow is difficult to attain and retain under most conditions of practical interest, e.g., on the surfaces of large transport airplanes. Laminar flow is an inherently unstable condition that is easily upset, and transition to turbulent flow may occur prematurely as a result of amplification of disturbances emanating from various sources. Two basic techniques are available to delay transition from laminar to turbulent flow—passive and active. Laminar flow can be obtained passively over the forward part of airplane lifting surfaces (wings and tails) that have leading-edge sweep angles of less than about 18 degrees by designing the surface cross-sectional contour so that the local pressure initially decreases over the surface in the direction from the leading edge towards the trailing edge. The laminar flow obtained in this passive manner is called natural laminar flow (NLF). In the rearward region of well-designed wings, where the pressure must increase with distance towards the trailing edge (an adverse pressure gradient),[1] active laminar-flow control must be used. Even in a favorable pressure gradient, active laminar-flow control is required to attain laminar flow to large distances from the leading edge.

The principal types of active laminar-flow control are surface cooling (in air) and removal of a small amount of the boundary-layer air by suction through porous materials, multiple narrow surface slots, or small perforations. For highly swept wings that are usually required for flight at high subsonic and supersonic speeds, only suction can control sweep-induced crossflow disturbances that promote boundary-layer transition from laminar to turbulent flow. The use of suction has become the general method of choice for active laminar-flow control and has become known as LFC. A combination of LFC (in regions where pressure gradients due to the sweep introduce large destabilizing crossflow disturbances) and NLF (in regions with low crossflow) is an approach to simplifying the application of LFC and is known as hybrid LFC (HLFC). Although the potential performance gains due to HLFC are somewhat lower than those obtainable with LFC, the gains are still very large.

At this point, a brief description of a parameter of fundamental importance is necessary for the non-technical reader. This parameter is called Reynolds number and was named after Osborne Reynolds who, in 1888, was the first to show visually the transition from laminar to turbulent flow and the complete mixing of the fluid elements in turbulent flow. Reynolds number is non-dimensional and is equal to the product of the velocity of a body passing through a fluid (v), the density of the fluid (ρ) and a representative length (l) divided by the fluid viscosity (μ) or $v\,\rho\,l\,/\mu$. Engineers select various representative lengths (l) in the formulation of the Reynolds number for different purposes. For example, non-dimensionalized aerodynamic forces acting on a body moving through air vary with the value of the Reynolds number based on the body length. This phenomenon is called "scale effect" and is important in the determination of the non-dimensional aerodynamic forces acting on a full-size (full-scale) airplane or airplane component from data measured on a small wind-tunnel model. When engineers select the distance from the component's leading edge to the end of laminar flow as the representative length, the resultant length Reynolds number (or transition Reynolds number) is a measure of the distance from the leading edge to the end of the laminar flow. For any value of transition Reynolds number, then, that has been experimentally determined, the distance to the end of laminar flow on any size airplane component can be calculated for any stream-flow velocity, density, and viscosity from the above Reynolds number formulation. The attainable value of transition Reynolds number, as previously indicated, is dependent upon the component's geometrical shape (the primary controller of the variation of surface pressure), various disturbances, and the type and magnitude of laminar-flow control used.

This monograph will review the history of the development of LFC and HLFC with emphasis on experimentation, especially flight research. A sufficient number of activities up to 1965, when a 10-year hiatus in U.S. experimental LFC research began, will illustrate the early progress as well as the principal problems that inhibited the attainment of laminar flow in flight with either passive or active laminar-flow control. Discussion of a resurgence of research on LFC in 1975 will concentrate on the flight-research portion of an American program defined to solve the technological problems uncovered during the previous research. Included will be a discussion of the significance of aircraft size on the applicability of passive or active control.

---

1 A decreasing pressure in the direction towards the trailing edge is called a favorable pressure gradient and an increasing pressure is called an adverse pressure gradient.

Early Research on Suction-Type Laminar-Flow Control

Research from the 1930s through the War Years

The earliest known experimental work on LFC for aircraft was done in the late 1930s and the 1940s, primarily in wind tunnels.[2] In 1939, research engineers at the Langley Memorial Aeronautical Laboratory of the National Advisory Committee for Aeronautics (NACA) in Hampton, Virginia, tested the effect on boundary-layer transition of suction through slots in the surfaces of wind-tunnel models. These tests provided the first aerodynamic criteria on the design of multiple suction slots and obtained laminar flow up to a length Reynolds number of 7 million, a phenomenally large value at that time. The first LFC flight experiments ever made followed these favorable results in 1941. Researchers installed seventeen suction slots between 20 and 60 percent of the chord[3] of a test panel (glove)[4] on a wing of a B-18 airplane (Figure 1). Maximum airplane speed and constraint in the length of the

Figure 1. B-18 airplane with test glove for natural laminar flow and later for active laminar-flow control. (NASA photo L-25336)

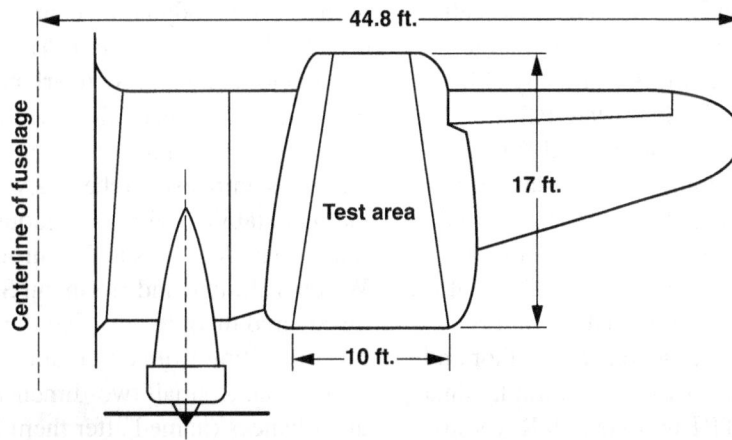

---

2 Three citations that provide extensive bibliographies on both passive and active control of the laminar boundary layer are: Dennis M. Bushnell and Mary H. Tuttle, *Survey and Bibliography on Attainment of Laminar Flow Control in Air Using Pressure Gradient and Suction* (Washington, DC: NASA RP-1035, September 1979); Charles E. Jobe, *A Bibliography of AFFDL/FXM Reports on Laminar Flow Control* (U.S. Air Force: AFFDL-TM-76-26-FXM, March 1976); and Mary H. Tuttle and Dal V. Maddalon, *Laminar Flow Control (1976-1991) – A Comprehensive, Annotated Bibliography* (Washington, DC: NASA TM 107749, March 1993). Significant references, primarily of summary natures, that were published since these are included in subsequent footnotes. A sparse number of technical sources already included in the bibliographies are also repeated in subsequent notes to assist readers in locating pertinent technical information discussed in the narrative.

3 Chord is the length of the surface from the leading edge to the trailing edge.

4 A glove is a special section of an airplane's lifting surface, usually overlaying the basic wing structure, that is designed specifically for research purposes.

wing glove, however, limited achievement of a length Reynolds number for transition to a value lower than that achieved in the wind tunnel.

Experimentation in NACA on LFC ceased during the years of World War II in order to develop natural laminar-flow airfoils, the so-called NACA 6- and 7-series airfoils, under the leadership of Eastman N. Jacobs, Ira H. Abbott, and Albert E. von Doenhoff at the Langley Memorial Aeronautical Laboratory.[5] Significant progress in furthering the understanding of the boundary-layer transition process, however, continued to be made in the U.S.A., both analytically and experimentally, principally at the National Bureau of Standards by G.B. Schubauer, H.K. Skramstad, P.S. Klebanoff, K.P. Tidstrom, and Hugh L. Dryden.[6] Development of the laminar-flow airfoils was made possible by the introduction into service of the Low-Turbulence Pressure Tunnel (LTPT) at the LaRC with an exceptionally low airstream-turbulence level.[7] The author and Frank Visconti measured natural laminar flow in the LTPT up to length Reynolds numbers on the order of 16 million.[8]

Researchers in Great Britain obtained significant flight experience in the mid-1940s on natural laminar-flow airfoils with wing gloves on the British King Cobra and Hurricane military fighters.[9] Large extents of laminar flow were obtained, but only after considerable effort to attain wave-free and smooth surfaces. Although attainment of large regions of laminar flow was not possible in daily operations, aircraft designers used laminar-flow type airfoils with large regions of favorable pressure gradient on new aircraft intended for high-subsonic-speed flight because of their superior high-speed aerodynamic characteristics, e.g., the North American P-51 Mustang.

In Germany and Switzerland, efforts to develop LFC technology with suction were under way during the war. The Germans emphasized the analysis of laminar stability with continuous suction rather than discrete suction through slots. Walter Tollmien and Hermann Schlichting discovered theoretically that the boundary layer resulting from continuous suction is very stable to small two-dimensional type disturbances (named after them as Tollmien-Schlichting waves)[10] and that

---

5 In a later reorganization, the Langley Memorial Aeronautical Laboratory was renamed the Langley Research Center (LaRC), and that name will be used hereafter to avoid possible confusion. An interim name for the Laboratory from 1948 to 1958 was the Langley Aeronautical Laboratory.

6 Dryden later became the Director of the NACA and then the first Deputy Administrator of the National Aeronautics and Space Administration (NASA).

7 A low level of high-frequency airstream turbulence, a condition approximating that in the atmosphere, is required to obtain natural laminar flow. This turbulence, of extreme importance to NLF, contrasts with occasional low-frequency turbulence in the atmosphere, known as gusts. Gusts affect an aircraft through changes in the relative angle of the aircraft with respect to the direction of flight (angle of attack).

8 Albert L. Braslow and Fioravante Visconti, *Investigation of Boundary-Layer Reynolds Number for Transition on an 65(215)—114 Airfoil in the Langley Two-Dimensional Low-Turbulence Pressure Tunnel* (Washington, DC: NACA TN 1704, October, 1948).

9 See, for example: W.E. Gray and P.W.J. Fullam, *Comparison of Flight and Tunnel Measurements of Transition on a Highly Finished Wing (King Cobra)* (RAE Report Aero 2383, 1945); F. Smith and D. Higton, *Flight Tests on King Cobra FZ. 440 to Investigate the Practical Requirements for the Achievement of Low Profile Drag Coefficients on a "Low Drag" Aerofoil* (British A.R.C., R and M 2375, 1950); R.H. Plascoff, *Profile Drag Measurements on Hurricane II z. 3687 Fitted with Low-Drag Section Wings* (RAE Report Aero 2153, 1946).

10 Examples of two-dimensional type disturbances are stream turbulence, noise, and surface irregularities having large ratios of width (perpendicular to the stream flow direction) to height, like spanwise surface steps due to mismatches in structural panels.

the quantity of air that must be removed to achieve this marked stabilizing effect is extremely small. German researchers derived methods for calculating the boundary-layer characteristics and drag reductions resulting from continuous suction. The Germans also wanted to validate their findings experimentally but were unable to produce a permeable surface suitable for continuous suction with the necessary degree of smoothness. Alternatives were tried, i.e., suction through a perforated plate and suction through multiple slots. Suction through perforated plates failed due to excessive disturbances emanating from the edges of the holes. Suction through multiple slots permitted attainment of extensive regions of laminar flow up to a length Reynolds number of 3.2 million. In Switzerland, Werner Pfenninger was also investigating the use of multiple suction slots. He obtained full-chord laminar flow on both surfaces of an airfoil but only up to a maximum chord (length) Reynolds number of 2.3 million. He attributed the limitation in the maximum attainable Reynolds number for laminar flow with LFC to increased airstream turbulence in the wind tunnel. From more recent results, he and other researchers agree that increased disturbances from small irregularities in the slot contours could have contributed.

Research from after World War II to the Mid-1960s

Release of the German LFC reports on continuous suction after the war generated renewed interest in both the United States and the United Kingdom.[11] The NACA initiated a series of wind-tunnel tests at the LaRC in 1946, which culminated in the attainment of full-chord laminar flow on both surfaces of an airfoil with continuous suction through a porous bronze surface. The author, Dale Burrows, and Frank Visconti obtained full-chord laminar flow to a length Reynolds number of about 24 million, which was limited only by buckling of the low-strength porous-bronze skin.[12] Neal Tetervin performed theoretical calculations indicating that the experimental suction rates were consistent with values predicted from the then-available stability theory to the largest chord Reynolds number tested. These wind-tunnel results, therefore, provided the first experimental verification of the theoretical indication that the attainment of full-chord laminar flow with continuous suction would not be prevented by further increases in Reynolds number, i.e., further increases in airplane size or speed (at least subsonically).[13]

Because porous bronze, however, was obviously unsuitable for application to aircraft (low strength and large weight) and no suitable material was available, work on the simulation of continuous suction with multiple slots was reactivated by the NACA. In the late 1940s, NACA researchers investigated in the LaRC LTPT an NACA design,[14] and Dr. Werner Pfenninger, who had come to the Northrop Corporation from Zurich, Switzerland, investigated a U.S. Air

11 A team of experts from the allied countries, including Eastman N. Jacobs of the NACA, gathered these reports in Germany soon after the end of hostilities.

12 This was the author's indoctrination into active laminar-flow control research, which followed previous involvement in the development of the NACA natural-laminar-flow airfoils.

13 Albert L. Braslow, Dale L. Burrows, Neal Tetervin, and Fioravante Visconte, *Experimental and Theoretical Studies of Area Suction for the Control of the Laminar Boundary Layer on an NACA 64A010 Airfoil* (Washington, DC: NACA Report 1025, 30 March 1951).

14 Dale L. Burrows and Milton A. Schwartzberg, *Experimental Investigation of an NACA 64A010 Airfoil Section with 41 Suction Slots on Each Surface for Control of Laminar Boundary Layer* (Washington, DC: NACA TN 2644, 1952).

Force-sponsored design.[15] In the first case, the researchers obtained full-chord laminar flow up to a Reynolds number of about 10 million (greatly exceeding that obtained previously in Germany and Switzerland), but the slot arrangement had been designed for a considerably larger Reynolds number of 25 million. In the second case, Dr. Pfenninger obtained full-chord laminar flow up to a Reynolds number of 16-17 million for a model designed for 20 million. In both of these cases with slots, as well as during the previous continuous-suction tests, an overriding problem in attainment of laminar flow was an increased sensitivity of laminar flow to discrete three-dimensional type surface disturbances[16] or slot irregularities as wind-tunnel Reynolds number was increased. This occurred in spite of the theory, which indicated that suction increased the stability of the laminar boundary layer with respect to two-dimensional type disturbances. More on this subject will be included later in the monograph.

After the war, the first work the British did on LFC was to extend the German analytical research on continuous suction. In 1948, Cambridge University experimented on a flat plate in the floor of a wind tunnel. This was followed in 1951 by flight tests on an Anson aircraft of continuous suction from 10- to 65-percent chord in a flat pressure distribution.[17] Researchers obtained experimental suction rates very close to theoretical values for a zero pressure gradient up to a length Reynolds number of 3 million and good agreement with theory in the measured boundary-layer profiles.[18] The experiments indicated adverse effects of roughness.

The British Royal Aircraft Establishment (RAE) tested a porous surface on a Vampire aircraft[19] starting in 1953 (Figure 2). Researchers initially employed a rolled metallic cloth for the surface, but roughness picked up in the mesh caused premature transition from laminar to turbulent flow. With the use of special procedures to provide very smooth surfaces back to 25 percent of chord, full-chord laminar flow was established at a length Reynolds number of 29 million. With candidates not yet available for a practical porous surface, attention was diverted to simulation of a porous surface with a perforated metal sheet. From 1954 to 1957, the RAE investigated various arrangements of hole size, spacing and orientation, as did John Goldsmith at the Norair Division of the Northrop Corporation in the United States. Some worked and some did not because of differences in disturbances generated by the suction flow through the different hole arrangements.[20]

---

15 Werner Pfenninger, *Experiments With a 15%-Thick Slotted Laminar Suction Wing Model in the NACA, Langley Field, Low Turbulence Wind Tunnel* (U.S. Air Force Tech. Rep. 5982, April 1953).

16 Three-dimensional type surface disturbances are those with width to height ratios near a value of one.

17 M.R. Head, *The Boundary Layer with Distributed Suction* (British A.R.C., R.&M. No. 2783, 1955).

18 A boundary-layer profile is the shape of the variation of a boundary-layer characteristic like local velocity or temperature with height above the surface.

19 M.R. Head, D. Johnson, and M. Coxon, *Flight Experiments on Boundary-Layer Control for Low Drag* (British A.R.C., R.&M. No. 3025, March 1955).

20 Significant sources are: John Goldsmith, *Critical Laminar Suction Parameters for Suction Into an Isolated Hole or a Single Row of Holes* (Northrop Corp., Norair Division Report NAI-57-529, BLC-95, February 1957); N. Gregory and W.S. Walker, *Experiments on the Use of Suction Through Perforated Strips for Maintaining Laminar Flow: Transition and Drag Measurements* (British A.R.C., R.&M. No. 3083, 1958). Northrop Corp., Norair Division reports cited in this monograph and others related to its laminar-flow research can be found in the files of Albert L. Braslow located in the Langley Historical Archives (LHA) at the Langley Research Center, Hampton, VA.

Figure 2. Vampire active laminar-flow-control flight experiments.

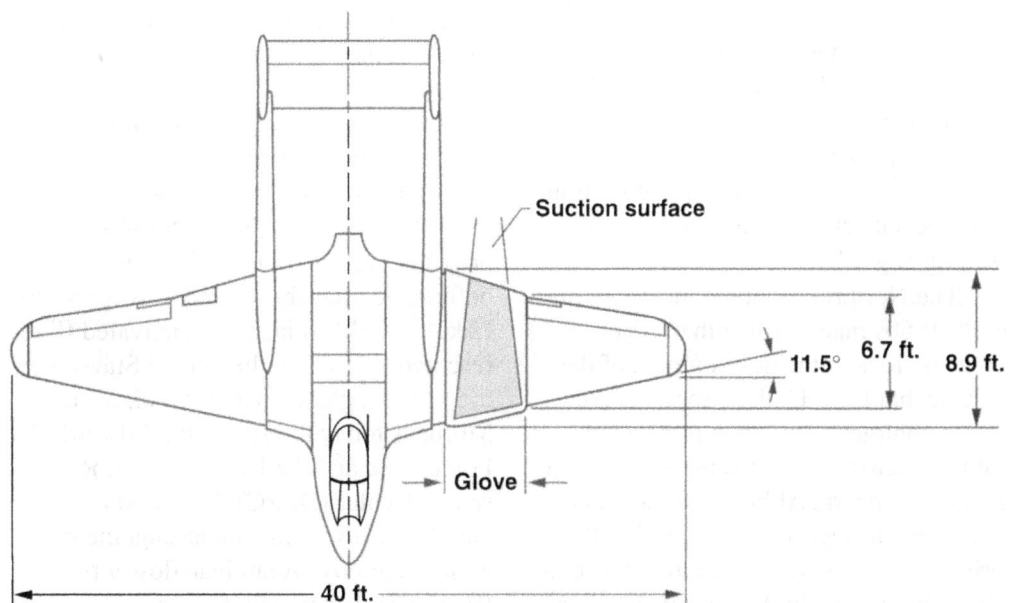

From 1951 to 1955, the British firm Handley Page tested, in wind tunnels and in flight on a Vampire trainer, the concept of suction strips whereby researchers hoped to eliminate the structural difficulties associated with fully distributed suction or with the need for precise slots. Tests included both porous strips and perforated strips with single and multiple rows of holes. The best of the perforated configurations consisted of staggered multiple rows of holes. Tests of porous sintered-bronze strips in both the wind tunnel and flight were troubled by great difficulty in ensuring sufficiently smooth joints between the strips and the solid surface. The joints introduced large enough two-dimensional type disturbances to cause premature transition. With the final perforation configuration, researchers obtained repeatable laminar flow to 80 percent of the chord on the Vampire trainer wing, equivalent to a length Reynolds number of 15 million. An inability to obtain laminar flow in the last 20 percent of chord was attributed to the effects of a forward sweep of the wing trailing edge.

Previously, in 1951, the RAE had been unable to obtain the design extent of laminar flow on a natural laminar-flow airfoil employed in a sweptback wing on an AW52 airplane. This led to a series of tests of sweptback surfaces of various aircraft during which visual records of boundary-layer transition were obtained. For sufficiently large leading-edge sweepback, transition occurred very close to the leading edge. Subsequent tests, using a flow-visualization technique, showed closely-spaced striations in the flow on the surface, indicating strongly that transition took place on swept surfaces as a result of formation of streamwise vortices in the laminar boundary layer.[21] Dr. Pfenninger's boundary-layer research group at the Norair Division of the Northrop Corporation in the 1950s provided a method of analyzing the cross-flow instability due to sweep. It also obtained experimental data showing that the cross-flow instability could be controlled by reasonable amounts of suction initiated sufficiently close to the wing leading edge.[22]

The Northrop group in the 1950s and early 1960s made many other major contributions to the development of the LFC technology. Under a series of Air Force contracts, the group performed rather extensive investigations in several areas of concern. Although some work was done on suction through holes, the principal efforts were on suction through slots. In addition to the improved understanding of laminar-flow stability and control on swept wings, the Northrop researchers developed criteria in the areas of multiple-slot design, internal-flow metering, and duct design plus techniques for alleviating the adverse effects of external and internal acoustic disturbances. In addition, Northrop conducted analytical investigations of structural design methods and construction techniques. These were supported by a limited effort on construction and test of small-scale structural samples. The results, however, were insufficient to provide transport manufacturers with confidence that LFC wings for future transports could be manufactured to the required close tolerances for LFC with acceptable cost and weight penalties.[23] An area receiving analytical attention only was that of the suction pumping system. Although the suction pumping system is of significant importance to overall aircraft performance, analyses indicated that no radically new mechanical developments were required to provide the necessary suction.

Northrop, in a USAF-sponsored program at Muroc Dry Lake (known both before and after this period as Rogers Dry Lake) in California, also reactivated flight research on LFC in the United States with the use of a glove on an F-94 aircraft. Muroc is today the site of the Edwards Air Force Base and the Dryden Flight Research Center (DFRC). Northrop investigated three different slot arrangements on a modified NACA laminar-flow airfoil (Figure 3). Essentially full-chord laminar flow was attained on the wing's upper

---

21 W.E. Gray, *The Effect of Wing Sweep on Laminar Flow* (RAE TM Aero. 255, 1952).

22 W. Pfenninger, L. Gross, and J.W. Bacon, Jr., *Experiments on a 30 Degree Swept, 12 Percent Thick, Symmetrical, Laminar Suction Wing in the 5-Foot by 7-Foot Michigan Tunnel* (Northrop Corp., Norair Division Report NAI-57-317, BLC-93, February 1957).

23 Structural design of airplanes requires consideration of manufacturing procedures, capabilities, limitations, and available materials as well as compatibility with in-service inspection, maintenance, and repair while providing a high degree of reliability and minimization of cost and weight. Airplane weight not only directly affects an airplane's performance but also its total life-cycle economics through its effect on construction costs, operating costs, and perhaps maintenance costs. The incorporation of laminar-flow control by suction imposes unique structural requirements in that smooth, substantially wave-free external surfaces are mandatory. Any associated additional weight or cost must not dissipate the advantages of LFC to a degree that the manufacturer or user would judge the remaining advantages insufficient to warrant the increased complexities or risk.

surface at Reynolds numbers over 30 million, the highest attained on a lifting wing. When the F-94 aircraft speed was increased to the point where the local Mach number[24] on the airfoil surface exceeded about 1.09, a new potential problem appeared. Full-chord laminar flow was lost with the slot configuration tested. This was probably due to the steep pressure rise through the shock waves that formed. Other data since that time, however, have shown that laminar flow can be maintained through some shock waves with a properly designed slot configuration. Another most important point is that for the F-94 glove tests, the airfoils were exceptionally well made with minimum waves and were maintained in a very smooth condition; even so, very small amounts of surface roughness, for example from local manufacturing irregularities or from bug impacts, caused wedges of turbulent flow behind each individual source of turbulence.[25]

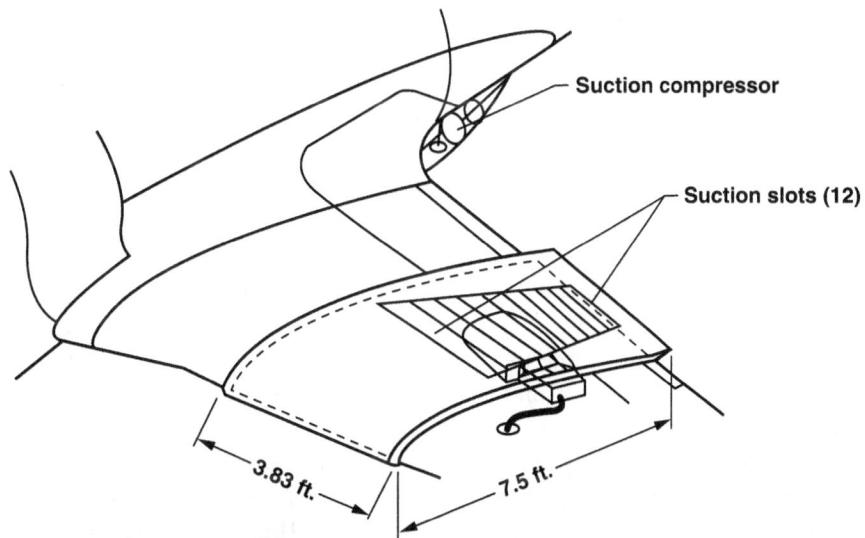

Figure 3. F-94 active laminar-flow-control flight experiments.

Suction compressor

Suction slots (12)

3.83 ft.

7.5 ft.

---

24 Mach number is a measure of airplane speed in terms of the ratio of the airplane speed to the speed of sound at the flight altitude. Airplane speeds up to the speed of sound are termed subsonic, above the speed of sound, supersonic, with the supersonic speeds greater than approximately Mach 5 (or 5 times the speed of sound) referred to as hypersonic. The region between about Mach 0.85 and 1.15 is termed transonic. Because of the cross-sectional curvature of lifting surfaces like wings, local Mach numbers of the air above the wing exceed the airplane Mach number.

25 W. Pfenninger, E.E. Groth, R.C. Whites, B.H. Carmichael, and J.M. Atkinson, *Note About Low Drag Suction Experiments in Flight on a Wing Glove of a F94-A Airplane* (Northrop Corp., Norair Division Report NAI-54-849, BLC-69, December 1954).

By this time, there was a better understanding that the use of increased air density in some wind tunnels, to more closely approximate full-scale flight values of Reynolds number, aggravated the surface roughness problem in the wind tunnel as compared with flight.[26] Nevertheless, the vast NACA experience in the development of laminar-flow airfoils in the late 1930s and early 1940s, the British flight tests of natural laminar-flow airfoils on the King Cobra and Hurricane airplanes in the mid-1940s, and the NACA and other previously mentioned tests of laminar-flow control through porous surfaces and slots in the late 1940s convinced the NACA that the inability to manufacture and maintain sufficiently wave-free and smooth surfaces was the principal impediment to the attainment of extensive regions of laminar flow for most airplane missions then conceived. The primary focus of the NACA (at least until its transformation in 1958 into the National Aeronautics and Space Administration [NASA]) was on the business of advancing the understanding of aeronautical phenomena and not on solving manufacturing or operational problems, which it considered to be the province of the manufacturer and user. The NACA, therefore, turned its attention away from LFC per se and concentrated its laminar-flow activities on expanding the understanding of the quantitative effects of surface roughness on transition, with and without suction. Based on these NACA data and pertinent data from numerous other researchers, a correlation was developed with which the permissible three-dimensional type surface-roughness height can be estimated within reasonable accuracy.[27]

NASA became aware in 1960 of a renewed U. S. Air Force (USAF) interest in active laminar-flow control through a visit of Philip P. Antonatos of the USAF Wright Air Development Division (WADD) to the author, who was then head of the General Aerodynamics Branch of the LaRC Full-Scale Research Division.[28] Contemplated Air Force missions at that time included a high-altitude subsonic aircraft of long range or endurance, an ideal match with laminar-flow control. Laminar flow was *required* to obtain the long range or endurance and high altitude alleviated the adverse effects of surface protuberances. Any special operational procedures needed to maintain the required surface smoothness in the presence of material erosion and corrosion and to cope with weather effects,[29] aircraft noise, and accumulation of dirt and insects could only be evaluated through actual flight experience. WADD also considered it important to provide an impressive flight demonstration of improved airplane performance to be better able to advocate the advantages of the contemplated new aircraft.

WADD proposed use of two WB-66D airplanes based on minimum cost, high degree of safety, and short development time. The Northrop Corporation, under sponsorship of the Air Force (with a monetary contribution from the Federal Aviation Administration),[30] later modified

---

26 The method of increasing the Reynolds number on small models in wind tunnels involves increasing the air density through an increase in air pressure (higher unit Reynolds number, i.e., Reynolds number based on a unit length). The minimum size of a three-dimensional type disturbance that will cause transition is smaller on a small model in an airstream of higher density than that required to cause transition on a full-size airplane at altitude (and, therefore, lower density) at the same relative distance from the leading edge.

27 Albert E. von Doenhoff and Albert L. Braslow, "The Effects of Distributed Surface Roughness on Laminar Flow," in *Boundary-Layer and Flow Control - Its Principles and Application*, Vol. 2, edited by G. V. Lachmann (Oxford, London, New York, Paris: Pergamon Press, 1961), pp. 657-681.

28 ALB files, LHA, notebook on Norair and LRC Memos re X-21: memo for LaRC Associate Director, 17 June 1960.

29 Weather effects include the effects of icing, precipitation, clouds, and low-frequency atmospheric turbulence.

Figure 4. One of two X-21 active laminar-flow-control airplanes.

these airplanes with slotted suction wings and designated them as experimental aircraft X-21A and X-21B (Figure 4). Beginning with the first development-engineering review of the X-21A in January 1963, the author acted as a NASA technical consultant to the Air Force.[31]

Northrop began flight research in April of 1963 at Edwards Air Force Base. Several problems arose early in the project that consumed significant periods for their solution. Principal among these was the old surface smoothness and fairness problem[32] and an unexpected severity of a spanwise contamination problem. With respect to the smoothness and fairness problem, in spite of a concerted effort to design and build the slotted LFC wings for the two airplanes to the close tolerances required, the resulting hardware was not good enough. Discontinuities in spanwise wing splices were large enough to cause premature transition. Putty, used to fair out these

discontinuities, chipped during flight with resulting roughness large enough to trigger transition.

The combination of X-21 wing geometry, flight altitudes, and Mach numbers was such that local turbulence at the attachment line, e.g., from the fuselage or induced by insect accumulation, caused turbulent flow over much of the wing span (spanwise contamination).[33] At about the same time, British flight tests of a swept slotted-suction wing mounted vertically on the fuselage of a Lancaster bomber indicated similar results (Figure 5).[34] Although flight experimentation and small-scale wind-tunnel tests by the British had previously indicated the existence of the spanwise-contamination problem, its significance had gone unrecognized. With the large-scale X-21 flight tests and further wind-tunnel tests, Northrop developed methods for avoidance of spanwise contamination. The phenomenon is now understood but

30 ALB files, LHA, notebook on Norair and LRC Memos re X-21: memo for LaRC Associate Director, 10 December 1963.

31 See ALB files, LHA, notebook on Norair and LRC Memos re X-21: memo to Air Force Aeronautical Systems Division from Charles J. Donlan, Acting LaRC Director, dated 2 January 1963, and for other memos and program reviews.

32 Surface smoothness is a measure of surface discontinuities like protuberances or steps. Surface fairness is a measure of the degree of waviness of surface contour (shape).

33 On a sweptback wing, the line at which the airflow divides to the upper and lower surfaces is called the attachment line. If the boundary layer at the attachment line becomes turbulent for any reason and if certain combinations of wing sweep, wing leading-edge radius, and flight conditions exist, the turbulence spreads outward along the attachment line and contaminates (makes turbulent) the boundary layer on both wing surfaces outboard of the initial turbulence.

34 R.R. Landeryou and P.G. Porter, *Further Tests of a Laminar Flow Swept Wing with Boundary Layer Control by Suction* (College of Aeronautics, Cranfield, England, Report Aero. No. 192, May 1966).

Figure 5. Swept, suction-type laminar-flow-control wing mounted vertically on Lancaster bomber.

requires careful attention in the design of large LFC aircraft.[35]

Another problem that was uncovered during the X-21 flight tests was associated with ice crystals in the atmosphere. Researchers noted that when the X-21 flew in or near visible cirrus clouds, laminar flow was lost but that upon emergence from the ice crystals, laminar flow was immediately regained. G.R. Hall at Northrop developed a theory to indicate when laminar flow would be lost as a function of atmospheric particle size and concentration.[36] Little statistical information, however, was available on the size and quantity of ice particles present in the atmosphere as a function of altitude, season of the year, and geographic location. Therefore, the practical significance of atmospheric ice particles on the amount of time laminar flow might be lost on operational aircraft was not known. By October of 1965, attainment of "service experience comparable to an operational aircraft," one of the program's

principal objectives, had not even been initiated because of the effort absorbed by the previous problems. To proceed with this initiative, the advisors to the Air Force recommended that a major wing modification would be needed before meaningful data on service maintenance could be obtained.[37] This, unfortunately, was never done because of various considerations at high levels of the Air Force, probably predominantly the resource needs of hostilities in Vietnam. Much extremely valuable information, however, was obtained during the X-21 flight program, supported by wind-tunnel and analytical studies. At the end of the program,[38] flights attained laminar flow on a fairly large airplane over 95 percent of the area intended for laminarization. Unfortunately, top management in government and industry remembered the difficulties and time required to reach this point more than they did the accomplishment.

35 W. Pfenninger, *Laminar Flow Control-Laminarization* (AGARD Special Course on Concepts for Drag Reduction, AGARD Report No. 654, June 1977).

36 G.R. Hall, "On the Mechanics of Transition Produced by Particles Passing Through an Initially Laminar Boundary Layer and the Estimated Effect on the LFC Performance of the X-21 Aircraft" (Northrop Corp., October 1964).

37 ALB files, LHA, folder labeled X-21 Tech Reviews: USAF Aeronautical Systems Division X-21 DAG Review Agenda and Attendees with Report of Review Group on X-21A Laminar Flow Control Program, 8 November 1965.

38 Special Section, "Laminar Flow Control Prospects," *Astronautics and Aeronautics* 4, no. 7 (July 1966): 30-62. This section contains articles by several different authors. On X-21, see also document 2 at the end of this monograph.

Post X-21 Research on Suction-Type Laminar-Flow Control

Hiatus in Research

With the cessation of military support, a general hiatus in the development of active laminar-flow control technology ensued in the United States from the mid-1960s to the mid-1970s. Other interest was lacking because of two principal reasons: 1) a lack of a contemplated need for very long-range missions for commercial aircraft for which the benefits of active laminar-flow control were a *necessity* and 2) the fact that the price of jet fuel was then so low that the estimated fuel-cost savings for commercial transports with ranges of interest was almost offset by estimated increases in manufacturing and maintenance costs. Researchers did perform significant analytical work and conceptual studies during this period, however.

Resumption of Research

In 1973, Gerald Kayten, who was Director of the Transportation Experiment Program Office in the Office of Aeronautics and Space Technology at NASA Headquarters, phoned the author with a request that he prepare a "white paper" on potential technology advances that might reduce the use of fuel by commercial air transports. The request was in response to increased prices and increasingly insecure sources of petroleum-based fuel resulting from the oil embargo imposed by the Organization of Petroleum Exporting Countries in 1973. NASA, at that time, was pursuing technological improvements in various aircraft disciplinary areas (identified and evaluated in the Advanced Transport Technology Systems and Design Studies)[39] to reduce aircraft noise

and pollution, to improve economics, and to reduce terminal-area delays. The resultant "white paper," printed December 20th of 1973,[40] recommended that the technological advances identified for these purposes be pursued with an increased emphasis on their potential for fuel reduction. It also identified additional possibilities in the aeronautical disciplines for fuel conservation. Principal among these, with by far the largest potential for fuel conservation of any discipline, was drag reduction through active laminar-flow control. Kayten, in a telephone conversation with the author on 14 January 1974,[41] called the paper "damn good," and he strongly urged that we get going quickly. He indicated, however, that the reception by others at Headquarters was nothing more than lukewarm. The same was true among LaRC researchers in management positions who believed that the problems previously evident in the laminar-flow research were so severe as to render the technology impractical and that any further efforts would only detract from the resources available for other research endeavors.

Because of this continued adverse reaction from many in positions of authority, start of a significant program on active laminar-flow control was continually deferred. Leaders of various groups during the next couple of years, however, initiated tasks to identify and recommend Research and Technology (R&T) activities that would be required to develop potential fuel-conservation technologies. The following are examples of the studies that resulted. In March of 1974, the American Institute of Aeronautics and Astronautics (AIAA) assembled a group of 91 of its members in a workshop conference. The objective was "to review

---

39 These studies were made under the Advanced Technology Transport (ATT) Program at LaRC under the direction of Thomas A. Toll.

40 Albert L Braslow and Allen H. Whitehead, Jr., *Aeronautical Fuel Conservation Possibilities for Advanced Subsonic Transports* (Washington, DC: NASA TM X-71927, 20 December 1973).

41 ALB files, LHA, chronological notebook on Advanced Technology Transport Office (later called Advanced Transport Technology Office and later changed in emphasis to Aircraft Energy Efficiency Project Office): note dated 1-14-74.

and discuss the technological aspects of aircraft fuel conservation methods and to recommend the initiation of those measures having the best prospects for short-term and long-term impact." One of the resultant conclusions was that advances in associated technologies since the 1960s warranted a reevaluation of the application of laminar-flow control in the design of future long-range transport aircraft.[42] In November of 1974, the Aeronautics Panel of the DOD/NASA Aeronautics and Astronautics Coordinating Board established a new subpanel on Aeronautical Energy Conservation/Fuels, cochaired by A. Braslow, NASA/LaRC and A. Eaffy, USAF/Pentagon.[43] The task was to "review the on-going NASA and DOD programs and recommend increased activities in fuel-conservation technologies where deficiencies were noted." The subpanel supported further research on LFC, including flight-testing.[44] Also recommended was the need for system-technology studies with fuel conservation as a primary criterion so that the application of the various technological advances could both separately and by interaction produce further significant fuel savings.[45] In 1975, NASA sponsored a Task Force of engineers from within NASA, the Department of Transportation (DOT), Federal

Aviation Administration (FAA), and Department of Defense (DOD) to examine the technological needs and opportunities for achievement of more fuel-efficient transport aircraft and recommend to NASA an extensive technological development program. The Task Force published its recommendations on 9 September 1975[46] and the Langley Director, Edgar M. Cortright, immediately established a Laminar-Flow-Control Working Group, chaired by the author, "to define a program of required R&T activities."[47] After definition of detailed plans and a process of evaluation, advocacy, and approval by NASA management, the U.S. Office of Management and Budget (OMB) and the U.S. Congress, the Task Force's recommendations evolved into the NASA Aircraft Energy Efficiency (ACEE) Program. The Office of Aeronautics and Space Technology (OAST) at NASA Headquarters managed the program.

The ACEE Project Office was established at the LaRC[48] to define, implement and manage three of six Program elements. The three elements were Composite Structures, Energy Efficient Transport (subdivided into Advanced Aerodynamics and Active Controls), and Laminar-Flow Control.[49] The acceptance of active

---

42 "Aircraft Fuel Conservation: An AIAA View" (Proceedings of a Workshop Conference, Reston, VA, 13-15 March, edited by Jerry Grey, 30 June 1974).

43 ALB files, LHA, folder labeled Aeronautics Panel, AACB, Energy Conservation/Fuels: Minutes of Special Meeting, NASA/DOD Aeronautics Panel, AACB, 11 November 1974, and Memorandum to Members of the Aeronautics Panel, AACB, 25 November 1974.

44 ALB files, LHA, folder labeled Aeronautics Panel, AACB, Energy Conservation/Fuels: Report of the Subpanel on Aeronautical Energy Conservation/Fuels, Aeronautics Panel, AACB, R&D Review, 5 December 1974, sect. 4.1.2. See document 1 at the end of this monograph.

45 Ibid., sect. 3.8.

46 *NASA Task Force for Aircraft Fuel Conservation Technology* (Washington, D.C.: NASA TM X-74295, 9 September 1975).

47 See document number 3 at the end of this monograph.

48 ALB files, LHA, Project Plan, Aircraft Energy Efficiency Program, Langley Research Center, L860-001-0, May 1976. Inserted is a page summarizing some key events.

49 Ralph J. Muraca was Deputy Manager for LFC to Robert W. Leonard, ACEE Project Manager in the LaRC Projects Group headed by Howard J. Wright. The author acted as Muraca's assistant.

laminar-flow control with suction (LFC) as part of the NASA ACEE program was based on the success of the previous experimental programs in attaining extensive regions of laminar flow on an operational airplane and more recent advances in materials and manufacturing technology that might make LFC more economically attractive. The principal motivation was the potentially larger gain in transport-aircraft performance resulting from laminarization of the boundary layer over wing and tail surfaces as compared with all other technological disciplines.

Formulation of the approved program received very extensive input and support from the air-transport industry.[50] An important example was the active participation of people from the industry in an LFC technology workshop held at the Langley Research Center on 6 and 7 April 1976.[51] Representatives of the airlines, manufacturers of large aircraft and aircraft engines, and individuals with expertise in LFC from the industry and government attended.[52] Objectives were to review the state of the art, identify and discuss problems and concerns, and determine what was necessary to bring LFC to a state of readiness for application to transport aircraft. The ACEE Project Office relied heavily on the discussions.

A change in LFC emphasis from the previous military application to the more difficult one of commercial transports, where manufacturing and operational costs are more important, made the LFC task even more challenging. The objective of the LFC element was to provide industry with sufficient information to permit objective decisions on the feasibility of LFC for application to commercial transports. It was expected that the

technology developed would be applicable to but not sufficient for very long-range or high-endurance military transports. The focus was on obtaining reliable information regarding the ability to provide and the cost of providing required surface tolerances as well as on the ability to maintain laminar flow in an airline operational environment. Improvements in computational ability for providing a reliable design capability were also of importance in the event practicality could be established. Implementation of the three project elements involved a major change in Agency philosophy regarding aeronautical research—a judicious extension of the traditional NACA research role to include *demonstration* of technological maturity in order to stimulate the application of technology by industry.

The ACEE/LFC project to bring active LFC from an experimental status to "technology readiness" for actual application required solutions to many difficult technical problems and entailed a high degree of risk—characteristics that dictated reliance on government support. A phased approach to require that progress in each area be evaluated prior to funding the next phase was accepted as a means of controlling the large resource commitments required and of alleviating the concern about the risk factor. This approach led to considerable heartburn in the project office in its attempt to complete a successful overall development in a timely fashion; a need to wait for successful results on intermediate steps was required before there could be adequate advocacy for the inclusion of subsequent phases in an annual government budget cycle. The project office

---

50 ALB files, LHA, notebook labeled Industry Comments: responses from industry top management to letter from Robert E. Bower, LaRC Director for Aeronautics, requesting response to five specific questions regarding LFC; internal ACEE Project Office memos on visits to industry to review detailed program proposals; and personal notes on trips to industry.

51 ALB files, LHA, Workshop on Laminar Flow Control held at LaRC, compiled by Charles T. DiAiutolo, 6-7 April 1976.

52 General chairmen were Adelbert L. Nagel and Albert L. Braslow of LaRC.

adopted the following guidelines for the LFC part of the program: "technology readiness" should be validated by the aircraft industry, and in particular, by those companies involved in production of long-range aircraft; the program should be cognizant of technological advances in other disciplines where those advances would be of particular benefit to LFC or where their application to future turbulent jet transports appeared likely; and the program should build on the existing data base, in particular, the USAF X-21 flights and associated programs previously discussed.

Research from the Mid-1970s to the Mid-1990s

For various reasons, the ACEE/LFC project required flight research in the following activities:

- Determination of the severity of the adverse effects of surface contamination by insects on the extent of laminar flow and the development and valida-

tion of an acceptable solution
- Evaluation of LFC surface and wing structural concepts employing advanced materials and fabrication techniques
- Development of improved aerodynamic and acoustic design tools and establishment of optimized suction criteria
- Validation of airfoil and wing geometries optimized for LFC
- Validation of high-lift devices and control surfaces compatible with LFC
- Demonstration of predicted achievement of laminar flow and validation of acceptable economics in the manufacture and safe commercial operation of LFC airplanes.

A few flight programs that investigated aerodynamic phenomena associated with attainment of natural laminar flow (NLF) provided information that was also of importance to active laminar-flow control at high subsonic speeds. These are discussed in the following subsections along with those that used LFC.

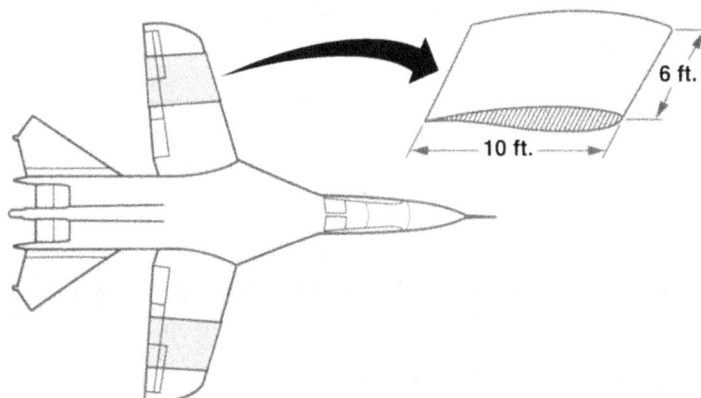

Figure 6. F-111/ TACT variable-sweep transition flight experiment. (NASA photo ECN 3952)

Natural Laminar Flow (NLF) on Swept Wings: F-111/TACT and F-14

Of principal significance in NLF flight research done with an F-111 airplane and an F-14 airplane was quantification of the adverse effect of crossflow instability due to wing sweep. Researchers installed supercritical, natural laminar-flow airfoil gloves on an F-111 aircraft (Figure 6), re-designated as the F-111/TACT (Transonic Aircraft Technology) airplane, and tested it in early 1980 at the Dryden Flight Research Center (DFRC)[53] through a range of sweep angles.[54] These results were limited by a restricted spanwise extent of the gloves, an abbreviated test schedule (caused by the required return to the Air Force of the borrowed aircraft), and limited instrumentation.[55] The results,[56] however, provided the basis for a follow-on program with another variable-sweep aircraft (an F-14 on loan to NASA from the Navy, Figure 7) that enabled attainment of a much broader and more accurate transition database. The F-14 research began in 1984 at the DFRC and was completed in 1987.[57]

Flush static-pressure orifices and

Figure 7. F-14 variable-sweep transition flight experiment. (NASA photo)

---

53 From 1981 to 1994, Dryden was subordinated to the NASA Ames Research Center as the Ames-Dryden Flight Research Facility, but to avoid confusion I will refer to it as DFRC throughout the narrative.

54 NASA flight-test participants were: Einar K. Enevoldson and Michael R. Swann, research pilots; Lawrence J. Caw followed by Louis L. Steers, project managers; Ralph G. (Gene) Blizzard, aircraft crew chief; and Robert R. Meyer, Jr., followed by Louis L. Steers, DFRC principal investigators. For an example of a flight report on the F-111 with the NLF gloves, see document 5 at the end of this monograph.

55 ALB files, LHA, folder labeled SASC 1980-81: memo on Natural Laminar Flow Flight Tests At DFRC On F-111 Aircraft, August 1980.

56 Boeing Commercial Airplane Company, Preliminary Design Department, *F-111 Natural Laminar Flow Glove Flight Test Data Analysis and Boundary Layer Stability Analysis* (Washington, DC: NASA Contractor Report 166051, January 1984).

57 NASA flight-test participants were: Edward T. Schneider and C. Gordon Fullerton, research pilots; Jenny Baer-Riedhart, project manager; Bill McCarty, aircraft crew chief; Harry Chiles, instrumentation engineer; Robert R. Meyer, Jr., chief engineer; Marta R. Bohn-Meyer, operations engineer; Bianca M. Trujillo, DFRC principal investigator; and Dennis W. Bartlett, LaRC principal investigator.

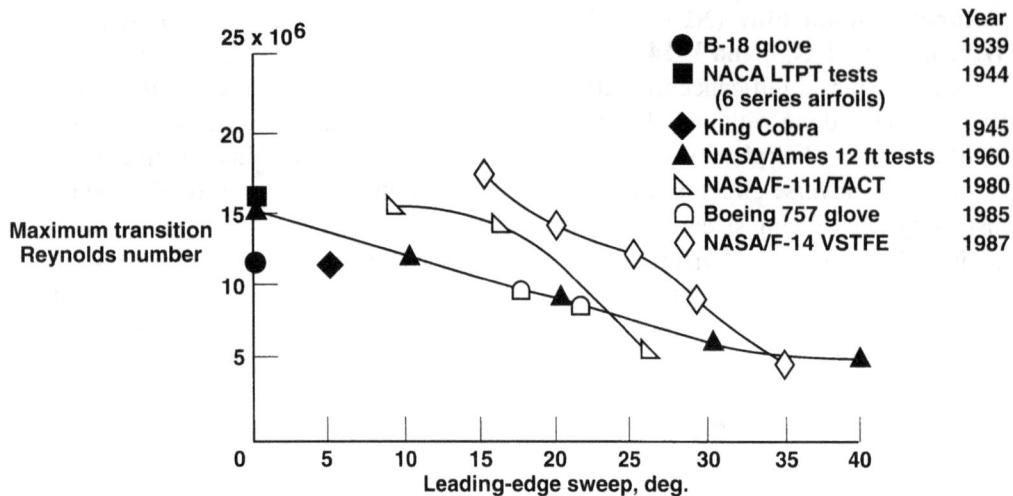

Figure 8. Maximum transition Reynolds number as a function of wing sweep.

surface arrays of hot films[58] were distributed over gloves with a different airfoil contour on each wing to determine local wing pressures and transition locations. Data from these sources and associated flight parameters were telemetered to the ground and monitored in real time by the flight-research engineer. Figure 8 presents results from the F-111 and F-14 swept-wing flight research along with results from low-speed wind-tunnel research in the LaRC Low-Turbulence Pressure Tunnel (previously mentioned in the Early Research section) and the Ames Research Center 12-Foot Tunnel. The results are presented as the variation of the maximum transition Reynolds number with wing leading-edge sweep. The research engineers, after careful consideration of the differences in accuracy of the various data, have judged that the extent of laminar flow (a direct function of the transition Reynolds number) is unaffected by wing sweep up to a value of about 18 degrees. At higher sweep angles, the extent of laminar flow is appreciably reduced by crossflow disturbances. The

F-14 transition data also provided sufficient detailed information to improve the understanding of the combined effects of wing cross-sectional shape, wing sweep, and boundary-layer suction (even though suction was not used on the F-14) on the growth of two-dimensional and crossflow disturbances.[59] This improved understanding permits a significant increase in maximum transition Reynolds number through the use of suction in only the leading-edge region of swept wings in combination with an extent of favorable pressure gradient aft of the suction, a concept called hybrid laminar-flow control (HLFC), to be discussed later.

Noise: Boeing 757

Under a NASA contract, the Boeing Company performed flight research in 1985 on the wing of a 757 aircraft (Figure 9) to determine the possible effects of the acoustic environment on boundary-layer transition. Because of a lack of sufficient data on the acoustic environment associated with wing-mounted high-bypass-ratio turbofan engines, a concern about

---

58 The hot-film sensors consisted of nickel-film elements deposited on a substrate of polyimide film with an installed thickness of less than 0.007 inch. Electric current is passed through the nickel elements and circuitry maintains a constant element temperature. The changes in current required to maintain the temperature constant are measured when changes in boundary-layer condition cause changes in cooling of the elements. The difference in cooling between a laminar and turbulent boundary layer and the fluctuating variations during the transition process from laminar to turbulent can then be measured and the transition location determined.

59 R.D. Wagner, D.V. Maddalon, D.W. Bartlett, F.S. Collier, Jr., and A.L. Braslow, "Laminar Flow Flight Experiments," from *Transonic Symposium: Theory, Application, and Experiment* held at Langley Research Center (Washington, DC: NASA CP 3020, 1988).

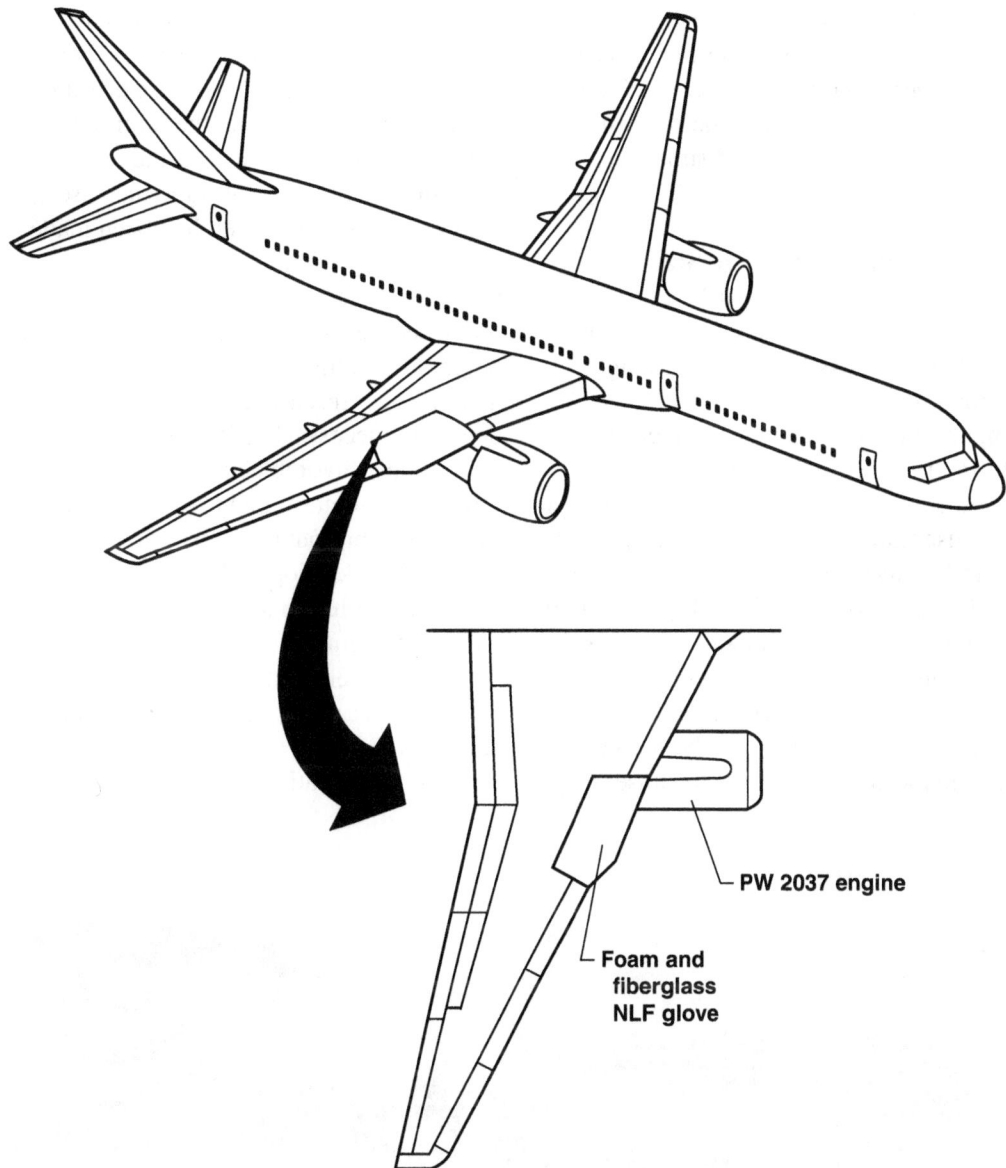

Figure 9. 757 transport noise experiments.

PW 2037 engine

Foam and fiberglass NLF glove

potential adverse effects of engine noise led to a belief that the engines needed to be located in an aft position on the fuselage. This location has a potentially severe adverse impact on performance and LFC fuel savings. Boeing replaced a leading-edge slat just outboard of the wing-mounted starboard engine with a 10-foot span smooth NLF glove swept back 21 degrees. Seventeen microphones were distributed over the upper and lower surfaces to measure the overall sound pressure levels, and hot films were used to measure the position of transition from laminar to turbulent flow. The starboard engine was throttled from maximum continuous thrust to idle at altitudes of 25 to 45 thousand feet and cruise speeds of Mach 0.63 to 0.83.

Although this flight research was not expected to provide answers on noise effects for all combinations of pertinent parameters, it did provide important indications. The most important was that engine noise does not appear to have a significant effect on crossflow distur- bances so that if the growth of crossflow disturbances in the leading edge is controlled by suction, large extents of laminar flow should be possible even in the presence of engine noise. If, however, in an HLFC application, the growth of two-dimensional type disturbances is comparable to or greater than the growth of crossflow disturbances, engine noise might be a more significant factor. The results were unable to validate theoretical predictions of the magnitude of noise levels at high altitudes and subsonic cruise speeds.[60]

Insect Contamination: JetStar

A major concern regarding the dependability of laminar flow in flight involved the possibility (most thought, probability) that the remains of insect impacts on component leading edges during flight at low altitudes during takeoff or landing would be large enough to cause transition of the boundary layer from laminar to turbulent during cruise flight. As a first step, the LaRC measured the insect remains that had accumulated on the leading edges of several jet airplanes based at the Center. The Langley researchers calculated that the insect remains were high enough to cause

transition, even at altitudes as high as 40,000 feet.[61] (Remember that an increase in altitude alleviates the adverse effect of surface roughness in that the minimum height of roughness that will induce transition increases as altitude increases.) An observation, however, had been made previously by Handley Page in England where flight tests of a Victor jet indicated that insect remains eroded to one-half their height after a high-altitude cruise flight. The Langley researchers, therefore, deemed it necessary to investigate further the possible favorable erosion but, if erosion was determined to be insufficient to alleviate premature transition at cruise altitudes, to develop and validate an acceptable solution to the insect contamination problem.

Researchers at the DFRC and the LaRC used a JetStar airplane at Dryden (Figure 10) in 1977 to investigate the insect-contamination problem.[62] With

Figure 10. JetStar aircraft and research team for investigation of insect contamination . Left to right: back row — Thomas C. McMurtry, test pilot; Kenneth Linn, instrumentation technician; Robert S. Baron, project manager; Donald L. Mallick, test pilot; Walter Vendolski, aircraft mechanic; John B. Peterson, Jr., LaRC principal investigator; front row — Albert L. Braslow, LaRC; James A. Wilson, aircraft crew chief; William D. Mersereau, flight operations; David F. Fisher, DFRC principal investigator. (Private photo provided by author)

---

60 Boeing Commercial Airplane Company, *Flight Survey of the 757 Flight Noise Field and Its Effect on Laminar Boundary Layer Transition*, Vol. 3: *Extended Data Analysis* (Washington, DC: NASA CR178419, May, 1988).

61 The calculations were based on von Doenhoff and Braslow, "The Effects of Distributed Surface Roughness on Laminar Flow," pp. 657-681, cited in footnote 27.

62 Dave Fisher was principal investigator at DFRC, and Jack Peterson formulated the program under the direction of the author at the LaRC.

contract support of the aircraft manufacturer, the Lockheed-Georgia Aircraft Company, they modified the left outboard leading-edge flap. Five different types of superslick and hydrophobic surfaces were installed in the hope that impacted insects would not adhere to them. In addition, researchers installed a leading-edge washing system and instrumentation to determine the position of boundary-layer transition. Dryden research pilots first flew the airplane with an inactive washer system on numerous airline-type takeoffs from large commercial airports. They flew at transport cruise altitudes and then landed at DFRC for post-flight inspection. These early tests indicated that insects were able to live in an airport noise and pollution environment and accumulated on the leading edge. The insects thus collected did not erode enough to avoid premature transition at cruise altitudes. It is probable that insect impacts at the much higher transport takeoff speed, as compared with the slow takeoff speed of the previously mentioned Victor airplane, initially compresses the insects to a greater degree where further erosion does not take place. None of the superslick and hydrophobic surfaces tested showed any significant advantages in alleviating adherence of insects. The need for an active system to avoid insect accumulation, then, was apparent.[63]

Although researchers had considered many concepts for such a system over the years and had tested some, none had been entirely satisfactory. The results of the flight research using the leading-edge washer system that had been installed on the JetStar leading-edge flap showed that a practical system was at hand. The tests showed that keeping the surface wet while encountering insects was effective in preventing insect adherence to the wing leading edge. After insect accumulation

was permitted to occur on a dry surface spray could not wash the insect remains off the leading edge (somewhat akin to the inability of an automobile windshield washer alone to remove bug accumulation from the windshield). The pilots, named in Figure 10, had flown the airplane with the spray on at low altitudes over agriculture fields in an area with a high density of flying insects in order to give the wet-surface concept a severe test.[64] Supporting analyses at LaRC also indicated an acceptable weight penalty of a washer system equal to less than one percent of the gross weight of an LFC transport airplane.

Leading-Edge Flight Test (LEFT) Program: JetStar

Planning for a flight test program to provide definitive information on the effectiveness and reliability of LFC began at LaRC soon after approval of the ACEE Program. The Langley ACEE Project Office expended considerable effort in consideration of candidate flight vehicles. Representatives of the airlines and transport manufacturers strongly advocated the need for a test aircraft equal to the size of a long-range transport (as indicated in the question and answer session of the 1976 LFC Workshop, cited in footnote 51) to provide meaningful results with respect to aerodynamic, manufacturing, and operational considerations. Government managers applied equally strong pressure towards the selection of a smaller size for cost reasons. The Project Office eventually formulated a satisfactory solution that fulfilled both requirements. It decided to restrict the tests to the leading-edge region of a laminar-flow wing suitable for a high-subsonic-speed transport airplane because the most difficult technical and design challenges that had to be overcome

---

63 David F. Fisher and John B. Peterson, Jr., "Flight Experience on the Need and Use of Inflight Leading Edge Washing for a Laminar Flow Airfoil," AIAA Aircraft Systems and Technology Conference, Los Angeles, CA (AIAA paper 78-1512, 21-23 August 1978).

64 Details of these flight tests are included in *ibid*.

before active laminar-flow control with suction could be considered a viable transport design option were (and still are) embodied in this region. The external surfaces at the leading edge must be manufactured in an exceptionally smooth condition (smoother than necessary at more rearward locations) and must be maintained in that condition while subject to foreign-object damage, insect impingement, rain erosion, material corrosion, icing, and other contaminants. In addition, an insect-protection system, an anti-icing system, a suction system, and perhaps a purge system and/or a high-lift leading-edge flap must all be packaged into a relatively small leading-edge box volume. Most of these problems equally affect the concept of hybrid LFC and the concept of active laminar-flow control with suction to more rearward positions.

The Project Office then selected the same JetStar airplane that was previously used for the initial insect-contamination flight research. The test article would be dimensionally about equivalent to the leading-edge box of a DC-9-30 airplane, a small commercial transport, where solution of the packaging problems would provide confidence for all larger HLFC and LFC airplanes with suction to more rearward positions. Its choice, however, did not receive unanimous concurrence. Dr. Pfenninger, who was then employed by the LaRC, strongly objected to selection of an airplane with a leading-edge sweep as high as the JetStar's (33 degrees) because he expected greatly increased difficulty in handling the large crossflow disturbances that would be introduced.[65] The Project Office accepted the risk, however, after extensive feasibil-ity studies and technical evaluations of several candidate aircraft.[66]

Selection of the most promising approaches to satisfaction of LFC systems requirements for both slotted-surface and perforated-surface configurations was based on several years of design, fabrication and ground testing activities.[67] The Douglas Aircraft Co. and the Lockheed-Georgia Aircraft Co. were the major contributors to this activity. Unfortunately, the Boeing Co. did not participate initially because of a corporate decision to concentrate its activities on the development of near-term transport aircraft. Boeing became active in the laminar-flow developments later. Inasmuch as no clear-cut distinction existed at that time between multiple slots and continuous suction through surface perforations made with new manufacturing techniques (although continuous suction had aerodynamic advantages), the Project Office prudently decided to continue investigation of both methods for boundary-layer suction. The Lockheed-Georgia Aircraft Company installed a slotted configuration on the left wing, and the Douglas Aircraft Company installed a perforated configuration on the right wing. The leading-edge sweep of both wing gloves was reduced from the wing sweep of 33 degrees to 30 degrees to alleviate the crossflow instability problem somewhat. Figures 11-13 present illustrations of the airplane and the leading-edge configurations.

The design of the slotted arrangement represented a leading-edge region for a future transport with laminar flow on both surfaces in cruise flight and included 0.004-inch-wide suction slots (smaller than the thickness of a sheet of tablet

65 ALB files, LHA, pocket-size "Memoranda" notebook: entry dated 2 September 1976.

66 ALB files, LHA, folder labeled LaRC Internal Memos on LFC dated 12/3/75 to 11/16/78: Memo to Distribution from Ralph J. Muraca, Deputy Manager, LFC Element of ACEEPO on Feasibility Studies of Candidate Aircraft for LFC Leading Edge Glove Flight — Request for Line Division Support, 16 November 1978.

67 Albert L. Braslow and Michael C. Fischer, "Design Considerations for Application of Laminar-Flow Control Systems to Transport Aircraft," presented at AGARD/FDP VKI Special Course on Aircraft Drag Prediction and Reduction at the von Kármán Institute for Fluid Dynamics, Rhode St. Genese, Belgium on 20-23 May 1985, and at NASA Langley on 5-8 August 1985, in AGARD Rept. 723, *Aircraft Drag Prediction and Reduction* (July 1985): 4-1 through 4-27.

paper) cut in a titanium surface.[68] The slots that encompassed the wing stagnation line also served the dual purpose of ejecting a freezing-point depressant fluid film for anti-icing and for insect protection. During climb-out, these slots were purged of fluid and they joined the other

for a future transport with laminar flow on the upper surface only—an approach that can provide future transports with significant simplifying advantages at the expense of a somewhat higher drag. In the design of future transports with upper-surface suction only, the adverse effect of

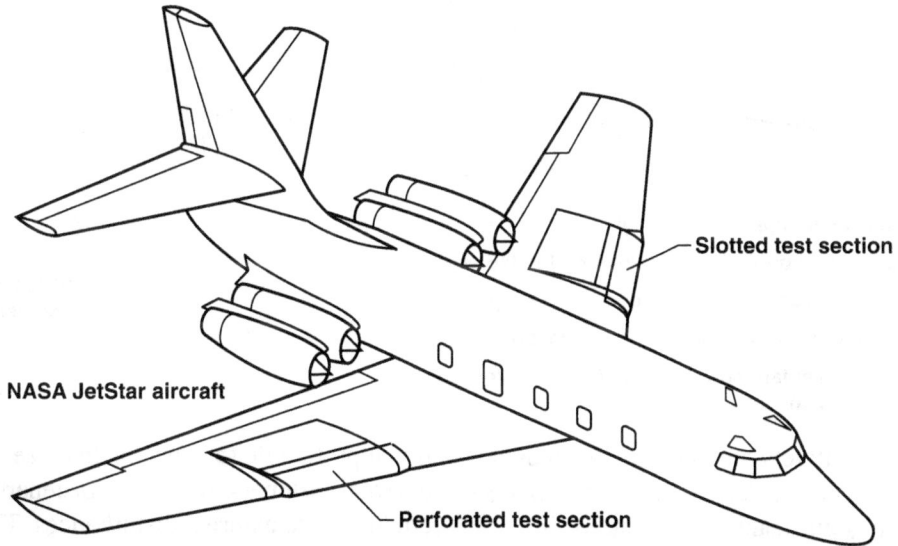

Slotted test section

NASA JetStar aircraft

Perforated test section

suction slots for laminarization of the boundary layer under cruise conditions.

The design of the perforated arrangement represented a leading-edge region

a loss in lower-surface laminarization will not be as great as one might expect because the skin friction is higher on the upper surface due to higher local veloci-

---

68 No leading-edge high-lift device was required for the transport aircraft conceptualized by Lockheed for this application of LFC.

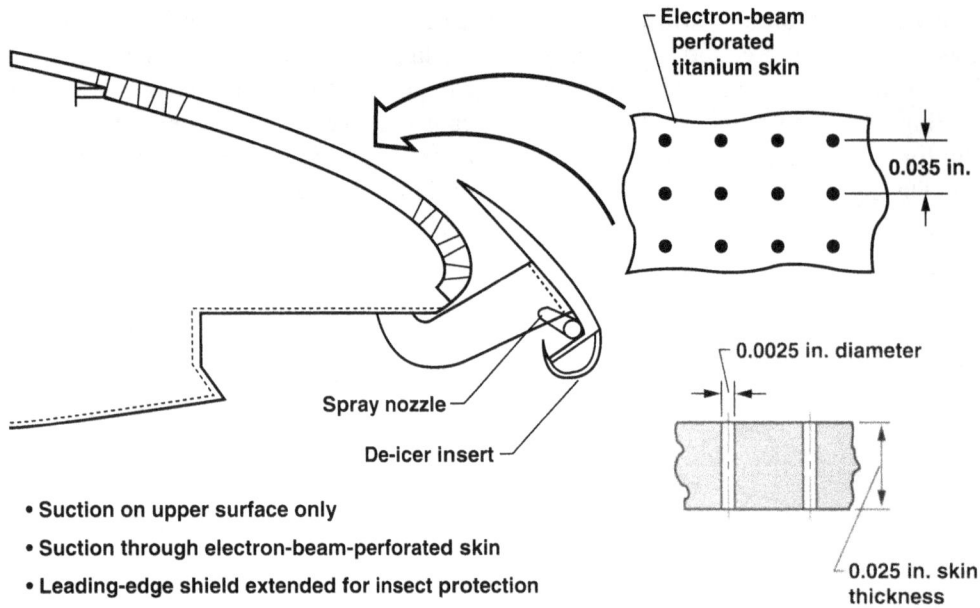

Electron-beam perforated titanium skin

0.035 in.

Spray nozzle

De-icer insert

0.0025 in. diameter

0.025 in. skin thickness

Figure 12. Leading-Edge Flight-Test program perforated test article.

- Suction on upper surface only
- Suction through electron-beam-perforated skin
- Leading-edge shield extended for insect protection
- De-icer insert on shield for ice protection
- Supplementary spray nozzles for protection from insects and ice

ties. A relatively small extension in upper-surface laminarization, therefore, can be used to significantly attenuate the increased drag of the lower surface.

The advantages of laminarization of only the upper surface include several features. Conventional access panels to wing leading- and trailing-edge systems and fuel tanks can be provided on the wing lower surface for inspection and maintenance purposes without disturbing the laminar upper surface. Laminarized surfaces in areas susceptible to foreign-object damage are eliminated. The wing can be assembled from the lower surface with the use of internal fasteners; this is

much preferable to concepts that use external fasteners, where the fasteners could induce external disturbances. The initial manufacturing costs and the maintenance costs are reduced. Upper-surface-only laminarization also will permit deployment of a leading-edge device for both high lift and shielding from direct impacts of insects. Deployment, when needed, and retraction into the lower surface, when not needed, will be permitted because the need for stringent surface smoothness on the lower surface will be eliminated. The test arrangement used such a device with an auxiliary nozzle to spray freezing-point

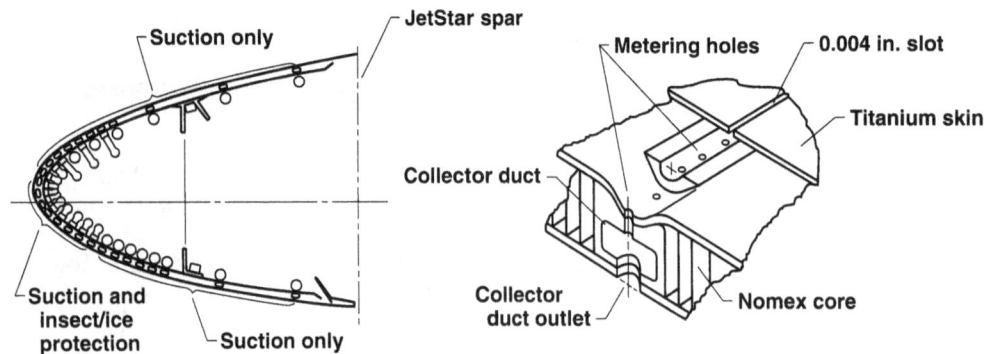

Suction only

JetStar spar

Metering holes

0.004 in. slot

Titanium skin

Collector duct

Suction and insect/ice protection

Suction only

Collector duct outlet

Nomex core

Figure 13. Leading-Edge Flight-Test program slotted test article.

- Suction on upper and lower surface
- Suction through spanwise slots
- Liquid expelled through slots for protection from insects and icing

24

depressant fluid for anti-icing and to provide conservatism in the elimination of insect adherence.[69] Finally, Douglas used a system for reversing the flow of air through the perforations on the test arrangement to remove possible residual fluid.

Use of electron-beam technology made possible, for the first time, manufacture of holes of a small enough size and spacing to avoid introduction of aerodynamic disturbances as large as those that had previously caused premature transition in wind tunnels. The successful use of laser "drilling" of holes followed later. The perforations in the test arrangement on the JetStar were 0.0025 inch in diameter (smaller than a human hair) and were spaced 0.035 inch apart in a titanium skin (over 4,000 holes per square foot of surface area). Only very close inspection would reveal a difference between a perforated-wing surface and a solid one.

In general, instrumentation was conventional but careful attention was required to avoid any adverse interference with the external or internal airflows. An unconventional instrument called a Knollenberg probe (a laser particle spectrometer) was mounted atop a ventral pylon on the fuselage upper surface to measure the sizes and quantities of atmospheric ice and water droplets. A charging patch, mounted on the pylon leading edge, provided a simple way to detect the presence of atmospheric particles and an impending loss of laminar flow by responding to the electrostatic charge developed when ice or water droplets struck the aircraft surface. The patch was investigated as a possible low-cost application to future laminar-flow airplanes.

The Dryden Flight Research Center again conducted the flight tests.[70] After initial tests to check out and adjust all systems and instrumentation, the principal effort focused on demonstration of the ability to attain the design extent of laminar flow under routine operational conditions representative of LFC subsonic commercial airplanes and on provision of insight into maintenance requirements. Simulated airline flights included ground queuing, taxi, take off, climb to cruise altitude, cruise for a sufficient time to determine possible atmospheric effects on laminar flow, descent, landing, and taxi. Conditions representative of airline operations included one to four operations per day and flight in different geographical areas, seasons of the year, and weather. Also, as in the case of commercial airline operations, the airplane remained outdoors at all times while on the ground and no protective measures were taken to lessen the impact of adverse weather or contamination on the test articles. In order not to increase pilot workload in the operation of LFC airplanes, the suction system was operated in a hands-off mode (except for on-off inputs).

All operational experience with the LFC systems performance (for both perforated and slotted configurations) during the simulated-airline-service flights was positive.[71] Specifically, during four years of flight testing from November 1983 to October 1987, no dispatch delays were caused by LFC systems. Laminar flow was obtained over the

---

69 After the early JetStar flight tests on the effectiveness of wetting the leading-edge surfaces for prevention of insect adherence, analyses and wind-tunnel tests of live-insect impacts were made by both Lockheed and Douglas to develop detailed arrangements of leading-edge-protection methods for their selected LFC configurations.

70 NASA Flight-test participants were: Donald L. Mallick and Fitzhugh L. Fulton, research pilots; Robert S. Baron, project manager; Ronald Young, instrumentation engineer; David F. Fisher followed by M.C. Montoya, DFRC principal investigators; and Michael C. Fischer, LaRC principal investigator. For background to the flight testing, see document 4 at the end of this monograph.

71 Dal V. Maddalon and Albert L. Braslow, *Simulated-Airline-Service Flight Tests of Laminar-Flow Control with Perforated-Surface Suction System* (Washington, DC: NASA Technical Paper 2966, March 1990).

leading-edge test regions as planned after exposure to heat, cold, humidity, insects, rain, freezing rain, snow, ice, and moderate turbulence. Removal of ground accumulations of snow and ice was no more difficult than the then-normal procedures for transport aircraft. No measurable degradation of the titanium surfaces occurred. Surface cleaning between flights was not necessary. Pilot adjustment of suction-system operation was unnecessary. The simple electrostatic "charging patch" device appeared to offer an inexpensive and reliable method of detecting the presence of ice crystals in flight (more about the atmospheric particle problem later).

The emergence of electron-beam perforated titanium as a wing surface that met the severe aerodynamic, structural, fabrication, and operational requirements for practical aircraft applications was considered to be a major advance in laminar-flow control technology by the principal government and industry investigators. Fabrication of the slotted-surface test article resulted in a suction surface that was only marginally acceptable, resulting in poorer performance. Some further development of slotted-surface manufacturing techniques, therefore, was (and is) still required. Also needed is proof of satisfactory aerodynamic performance of the perforated surface at larger values of length

Reynolds number, i.e., to distances greater than the end of the leading-edge test article. Nevertheless, the simulated-airline-service flights successfully demonstrated the overall practicality of baseline designs for leading-edge LFC systems for future commercial-transport aircraft, a major step forward.

Surface Disturbances: JetStar

In 1986 and 1987, the LaRC LFC Project Office, which had continued research on LFC after termination of the ACEE Project,[72] took advantage of the continued availability of the JetStar airplane at the DFRC to further the quantitative database on the effects of two- and three-dimensional-type surface roughness and on the effects of suction variations.[73] The most significant results that were obtained concerned clarification of the quantitative effects of crossflow due to sweep on the roughness sizes that would cause premature transition. As indicated many times in this monograph, the adverse effect of surface protuberances on the ability to maintain laminar flow was the primary inhibiting factor to the practicality of LFC. Although an empirical method of determining the quantitative effects of surface roughness on transition had been developed much earlier for unswept wings,[74] some indications had later become available[75] that wing sweep (crossflow effects) might

---

72 Richard D. Wagner headed the LaRC LFC Project Office during the 1980s (at first, still under ACEE) and was followed by F.S. Collier, Jr. The author, after his retirement from NASA in 1980, continued to provide significant input into the planning, analysis and reporting of much of the experimental research and development activities through local aerospace contractors. Dal V. Maddalon was technical monitor for these contracts. See ALB files, four folders labeled SASC (Systems and Applied Sciences Corporation) and one folder labeled Analytical Services and Materials, Inc. (April, 1980 through Sept., 1993).

73 Dal V. Maddalon, F.S. Collier, Jr., L.C. Montoya, and C.K. Land, "Transition Flight Experiments on a Swept Wing with Suction" (AIAA paper 89-1893, 1989); Albert L. Braslow and Dal V. Maddalon, *Flight Tests of Three-Dimensional Surface Roughness in the High-Crossflow Region of a Swept Wing with Laminar-Flow Control* (Washington, DC: NASA TM 109035, October 1993); Albert L. Braslow and Dal V. Maddalon, *Flight Tests of Surface Roughness Representative of Construction Rivets on a Swept Wing with Laminar-Flow Control* (Washington, DC: NASA TM 109103, April 1994).

74 See von Doenhoff and Braslow, "The Effects of Distributed Surface Roughness on Laminar Flow," pp. 657-681, cited in footnote 27.

75 Dezso George-Falvy, "In Quest of the Laminar-Flow Airliner—Flight Experiments on a T-33 Jet Trainer," 9th Hungarian Aeronautical Science Conference, Budapest, Hungary (10-12 November 1988).

exacerbate the roughness effects. Analysis of the additional JetStar data[76] indicated that the adverse effect of crossflow occurred for two- rather than three-dimensional type roughness.[77]

Figure 14 plots a roughness Reynolds number parameter against the ratio of roughness width to height.[78] The symbols represent data for unswept wings with no

type roughness (ratios of roughness width or diameter to height of approximately 0.5 to 5.0) located in a high crossflow region is the same as that previously established in zero crossflow; 2) only for more two-dimensional type roughness (roughness width to height ratios equal to or greater than approximately 24) will high crossflow decrease the permissible height

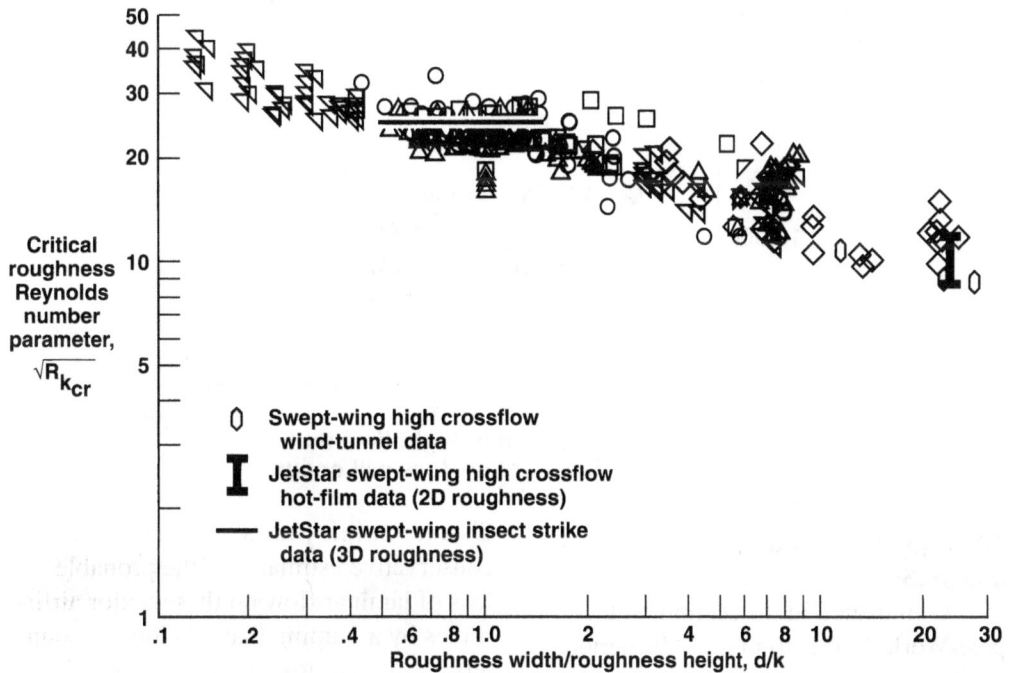

Figure 14. Comparison of swept-wing surface roughness data with unswept-wing von Doenhoff-Braslow data correlation.

crossflow except for a group of three identified for swept wings in high crossflow.[79] The vertical bracket indicates a range of roughness data obtained on the sweptback JetStar in a region of high crossflow. The horizontal line represents other roughness data obtained on the JetStar in both low and high crossflow. The important conclusions are: 1) for practical engineering application, the permissible height of three-dimensional

of roughness; and 3) for values of roughness width to height ratios equal to or greater than approximately 30, development of a different criterion for permissible roughness height is required. Information of this kind is crucial for the establishment of the manufacturing tolerances and maintenance requirements that must be met for surface smoothness.

---

76 From the second and third sources cited in footnote 73.

77 For any reader interested in a brief summary of the basic two- and three-dimensional roughness effects on laminar flow without crossflow, the discussion on pages 2-4 of the second citation in footnote 73 is recommended.

78 From Figure 7 of the third source cited in footnote 73.

79 See von Doenhoff and Braslow, "The Effects of Distributed Surface Roughness on Laminar Flow," pp. 657-681, cited in footnote 27.

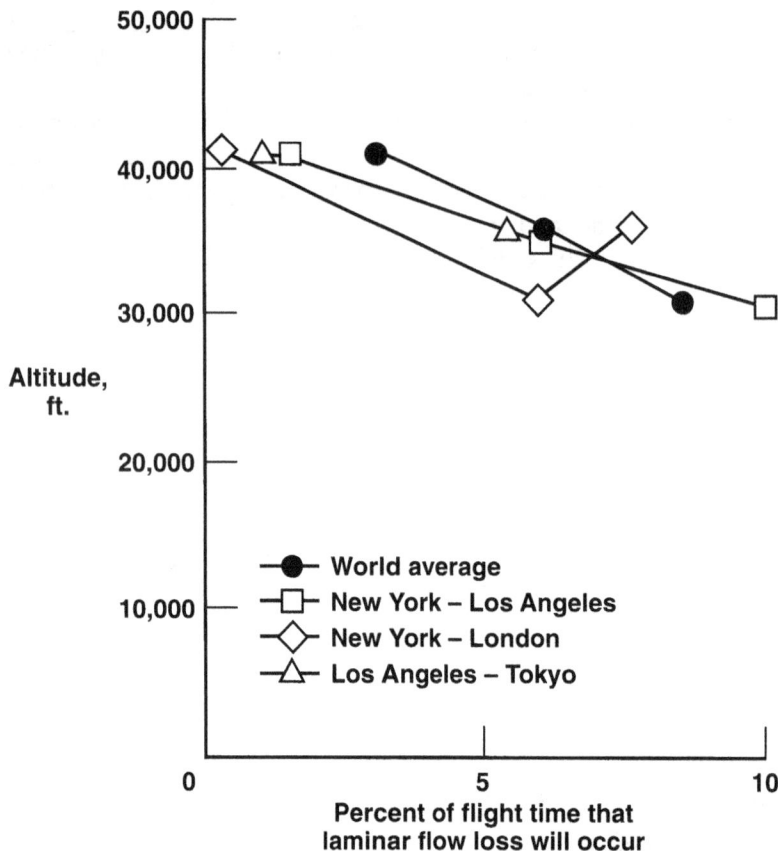

Figure 15. Potential laminar-flow loss on some major airline routes.

Atmospheric Ice Particles: Boeing 747s and JetStar

As indicated in the section on the post-World War II to mid-1960s period, the practical significance of atmospheric ice particles on the amount of time laminar flow might be lost on operational aircraft was not known because of a lack of information on particle concentrations. Unanalyzed cloud-encounter and particle-concentration data became available from the NASA Lewis Research Center (LeRC) Global Atmospheric Sampling Program (GASP) in the late 1970s. From March 1975 to June 1979, NASA obtained data with instruments placed aboard four 747 airliners on more than 3,000 routine commercial flights that involved about 88,000 cloud-encounters.[80]

With the GASP data, Richard E. Davis of the LaRC estimated average cloud-cover statistics for several long-distance airline routes. He then made conservative estimates of the probable loss of laminar flow on these major airline routes by assuming that all cloud encounters cause *total* loss of laminar flow, i.e., that the percentage loss of laminar flow on a given flight is equal to the percentage of time spent within clouds on that flight. For further conservatism, he assumed that pilots would make no attempt to avoid flight through clouds. Figure 15 is an example of the potential laminar-flow loss on some of the major airline routes—Los Angeles-Tokyo, New York-London, and New York-Los Angeles. The figure also includes a world average. These results now make it apparent that cloud encounters during cruise of long-range commercial air transports are not frequent enough to invalidate the large performance improvements attainable through application of LFC.

80 William H. Jasperson, Gregory D. Nastrom, Richard E. Davis, and James D. Holdeman, *GASP Cloud- and Particle-Encounter Statistics, and Their Application to LFC Aircraft Studies, Vol. I: Analysis and Conclusions, and Vol. II: Appendixes* (Washington, DC: NASA Technical Memorandum 85835, October 1984).

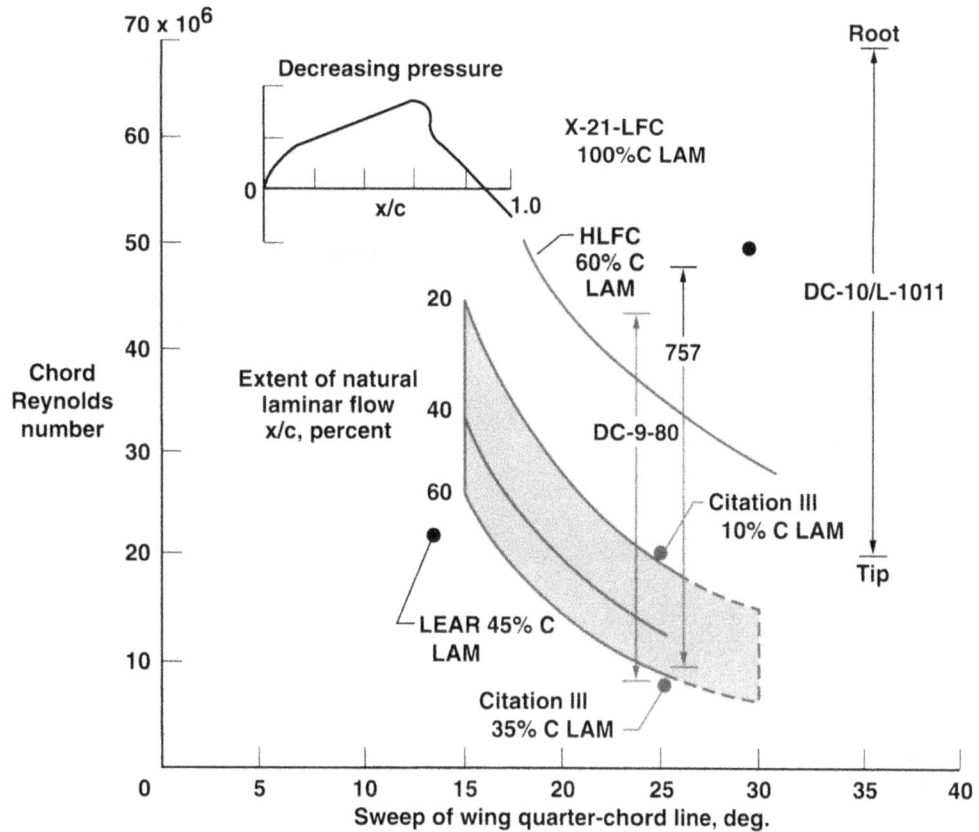

Figure 16. Possibilities of laminar flow on swept wings.

In addition, during the JetStar LEFT program, the Dryden flight-test team measured the size and concentration of atmospheric particles encountered at the same time they measured the degree of laminar-flow degradation. With these LEFT measurements, Davis at LaRC provided some validation of the Hall theory of laminar-flow loss as a function of atmospheric particle size and concentration.[81]

Hybrid Laminar-Flow Control (HLFC): Boeing 757

The hybrid laminar-flow control concept integrates active laminar-flow control with suction (LFC) and natural laminar flow (NLF) and avoids the objectionable characteristics of each. The leading-edge sweep limitation of NLF is overcome through application of suction in the leading-edge box to control crossflow and attachment-line instabilities characteristic of swept wings. Wing shaping for favorable pressure gradients to suppress Tollmien-Schlichting instabilities and thus allow NLF over the wing box region (the region between the two wing structural spars) removes the need for inspar LFC suction and greatly reduces the system complexity and cost.[82] HLFC offers the possibility of achieving extensive laminar flow on commercial or military transport aircraft with a system

---

81 See Hall, "On the Mechanics of Transition," cited in footnote 36.

82 Examples of additional complexities associated with suction over the wing box include: manufacture of a structural box of sufficient strength and light weight with slots or perforations over a much more extensive area of the wing skin; extensive internal suction ducting that decreases the internal wing volume available for storage of airplane fuel; larger suction pump(s) than otherwise needed; an increased difficulty in providing the required surface smoothness and fairness for maintenance of laminar flow over inspection panels in slotted or perforated surfaces when laminarization of both upper and lower surfaces is desired; and a need to avoid hazards due to possible leakage of fuel into the suction ducting. These complexities, along with other special features, increase airplane weight and manufacturing costs as well as maintenance costs.

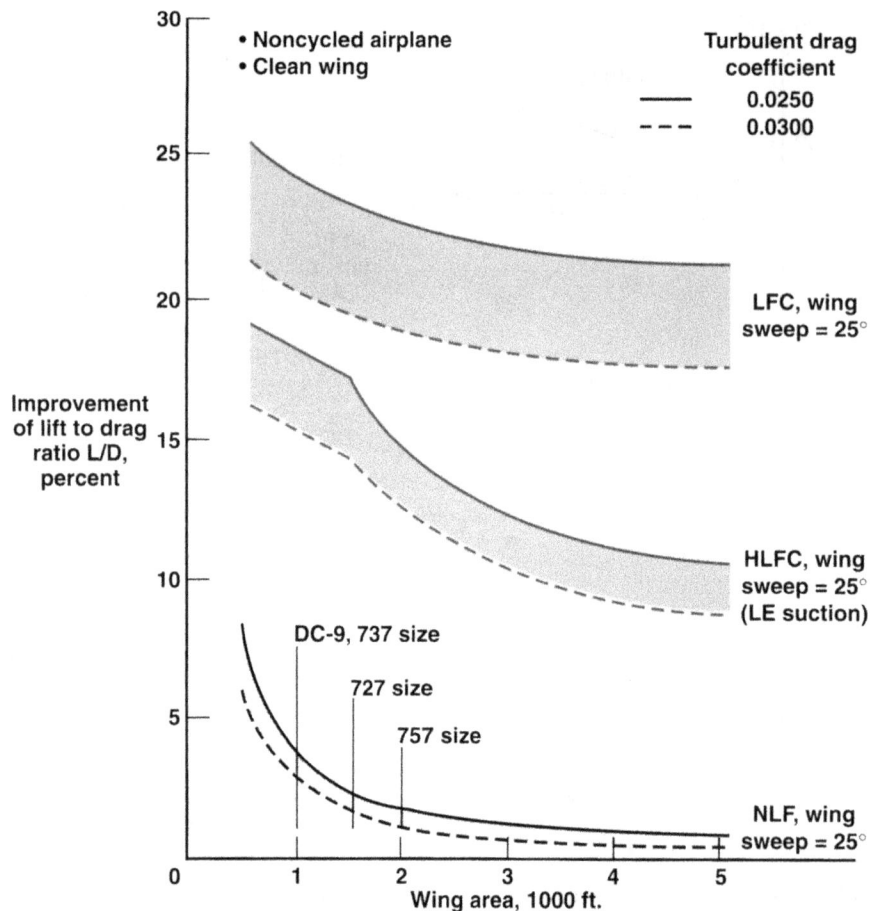

Figure 17. Improvement in lift-to-drag ratio due to laminar concepts.

no more complex than that already proven in the LEFT program on the NASA JetStar.

The relative place of HLFC, LFC and NLF in the wing-sweep-to-aircraft-size spectrum is indicated in Figure 16. On a grid of chord Reynolds number vs. quarter-chord sweep are plotted various items. The shaded area indicates the approximate chordwise extent of natural laminar flow attainable on a wing with initially decreasing surface pressures in the direction towards the trailing edge (upper left plot). Ranges of wing chord Reynolds number in cruise for four commercial transport airplanes are superimposed—for the Douglas DC-10, Lockheed L-1011, Boeing-757 and Douglas DC-9-80 airplanes. For each airplane, the wing chord Reynolds number decreases along the span from root to tip because of a taper in the wing planform.

The figure indicates that natural laminar flow can be attained only on

regions of the wings near the wing tips. As the wing-section chord increases (increased Rc) due to either a location nearer the wing root or an increase in airplane size, the chordwise extent of laminar flow decreases (due to increased Tollmien-Schlichting instabilities). Also, less laminar flow is attainable as the wing sweep increases (due to increased crossflow instabilities). The use of wall suction, however, permits the maintenance of laminar flow to large chordwise extents at both high sweep and large size (high Reynolds number), as indicated by the X-21 data point, but at the expense of complexities due to the extensive suction system. A combination of principles for active laminar-flow control and natural laminar flow—hybrid laminar-flow control (HLFC)—greatly increases the size of high subsonic-speed airplanes for which large extents of laminar flow can be obtained as compared with natural laminar-flow airplanes. For example, compare the chord Reynolds number for

Figure 18. 757 subsonic hybrid laminar flow control flight experiment. (NASA photo L-90-9549)

60-percent chord laminar flow with HLFC on the upper surface with the chord Reynolds number for natural laminar flow (of a smaller relative extent) on Citation III and Learjet airplanes, also plotted in Figure 16.

Figure 17 plots the percentage improvement of lift-to-drag ratio (L/D)[83] for each of the three laminar-flow concepts as compared with a turbulent airplane, plotted as a function of airplane wing area. The figure shows a large improvement in L/D for HLFC as compared with NLF. For the larger airplanes, of course, appreciably larger benefits are obtained with active laminar-flow control with suction to positions farther aft. As in the case of LFC farther aft, the concept of hybrid laminar-flow control requires smoothness of surface finish and contour as well as protection from insect residue and ice accumulation in the leading-edge region. The systems developed in the LEFT program for the leading-edge region are equally applicable for the hybrid laminar-flow control application.

Under a participatory arrangement between the LaRC, the USAF, and the Boeing Commercial Airplane Company, Boeing flight tested the effectiveness of hybrid laminar-flow control on a company-owned 757 airplane in 1990. Figure 18 shows an HLFC glove installed on a large section of the left wing. The systems in the leading-edge wing box are very similar to those flight tested on the JetStar airplane—a Krueger flap[84] for insect protection and high lift; a perforated titanium suction surface; and suction to the front spar with an ability to reverse flow for purging. Rather than use ejection of a freezing-point depressant, the design encompassed thermal anti-icing, i.e., reversal of the airflow and expulsion of heated air through the perforations in the leading-edge region. Boeing pilots flew the airplane at transport cruise Mach numbers and altitudes.

The primary goal was to establish the aerodynamics of HLFC at Reynolds numbers associated with medium-size transport airplanes to reduce industry

---

83 L/D is a significant measure of aerodynamic performance.

84 "Krueger" designates a specific type of leading-edge high-lift device (flap) that retracts into the wing lower surface. When used for an active laminar-flow control application, the flap also shields the wing from insect impacts during takeoff and landing and when retracted under the leading edge for cruise, does not interfere with the upper-surface laminar flow.

risks to acceptable levels. Results were very encouraging. Transition location was measured several feet past the end of suction and with less suction than estimated. The Krueger leading-edge flap proved effective as the insect shield. Existing manufacturing technology permitted construction of the leading-edge box to laminar-flow surface-quality requirements. All necessary systems required for practical HLFC were successfully installed into a commercial transport wing.[85]

Research engineers at the LaRC calculated the benefits of the application of hybrid laminar-flow control to a 300-passenger long-range twin-engine subsonic transport.[86] With what appear to be reasonable assumptions of 50-percent chord laminar flow on the wing upper surface and 50-percent chord laminar flow on both surfaces of the vertical and horizontal tails, HLFC provides a 15-percent reduction in block fuel from that of a turbulent transport.[87] Application of HLFC to the engine nacelles has the potential of at least an additional 1-percent block-fuel reduction with laminar flow to 40 percent of the nacelle length.[88]

Supersonic Laminar-Flow Control: F-16XL
In the late 1980s, the Laminar-Flow Control Project Office of the Langley Research Center reactivated a long-dormant consideration of LFC for commercial supersonic transports as part of a NASA technology-development program for high-speed civil transports. As is the case for subsonic flight, potential benefits of the application of LFC to supersonic transports include increased range, improved fuel economy, and reduced airplane weight. Reduced fuel consumption will not only improve economics but will also reduce a potential adverse impact of engine emissions on the earth's ozone layer from flight of supersonic airplanes at higher altitudes than those for subsonic flight. Additional benefits of reduced airplane weight at supersonic speeds are a decrease in the magnitude of sonic booms[89] and a reduction in community noise during takeoff.[90] Also, the lower skin friction of laminar boundary layers as compared with turbulent boundary layers is of even more importance at supersonic speeds than at subsonic speeds because the associated aerodynamic heating of the surface by the skin friction is an important design consideration at supersonic speeds.[91] The Boeing Commercial Airplane Company and the Douglas Aircraft Company of the McDonnell Douglas Corporation,[92] both under contract to the LaRC LFC Project Office, first studied needed aerodynamic modifications and associated structural and systems requirements to arrive at a realistic assessment of the net performance benefits of super-

---

85 A generally-available technical report on the HLFC flight tests has not been published.

86 Richard H. Petersen and Dal V. Maddalon, *NASA Research on Viscous Drag Reduction* (Washington, DC: NASA TM 84518, August 1982).

87 Block fuel is the fuel burned from airport gate to airport gate, excluding fuel burned due to any delays.

88 ALB files, LHA, P.K. Bhutiani, Donald F. Keck, Daniel J. Lahti, and Mike J. Stringas, "Investigating the Merits of a Hybrid Laminar Flow Nacelle, The Leading Edge" (General Electric Company, GE Aircraft Engines, Spring 1993).

89 The magnitude of a sonic boom is proportional to the airplane lift which is proportional to the airplane weight at a given cruise speed. If sonic-boom overpressures are reduced below a value of one pound per square foot, overland supersonic cruise may become allowable.

90 Takeoff noise is reduced by a reduction in takeoff thrust requirements resulting from lower weight.

91 Reduced aerodynamic heating increases material options, enhances the potential for unused fuel as a heat sink for airplane environmental control systems, and decreases the detectability of military aircraft.

Figure 19. Two-seat F-16XL Supersonic Laminar-Flow-Control flight research aircraft with a suction glove installed on the left wing. (NASA photo EC96-43831-5 by Jim Ross).

Suction glove

sonic-LFC implementation. Although promising conclusions were reached, the studies indicated the need for additional research and development specific to the supersonic application. Recommendations were made for supersonic flight research on HLFC.[93]

After additional analyses, wind-tunnel testing and exploratory flight research at the DFRC on two prototype F-16XL airplanes denoted as ship 1 and ship 2, DFRC also flight researched a laser-perforated titanium glove installed on the left wing of ship 2 (Figure 19).[94] Under LFC Project Office management, the Rockwell Corporation and the Boeing Company manufactured and installed the glove and the Boeing and Douglas Companies supported DFRC with

the flight research and analysis. Specific objectives were to determine the capability of active LFC to obtain a large chordwise extent of laminar flow on a highly-swept wing at supersonic speeds and to provide validated computational codes, design methodology, and initial suction-system design criteria for application to supersonic transport aircraft. To make accurate measurements, the investigators installed an extensive array of hot-film, pressure, and temperature instrumentation and provided real-time displays of the measurements. They completed thirty-eight flights with active boundary-layer suction and experienced very few problems with the suction system.[95] The laminar-flow data are currently restricted in distribution.

---

92 Now part of Boeing.

93 A.G. Powell, S. Agrawal, and T.R. Lacey, *Feasibility and Benefits of Laminar Flow Control on Supersonic Cruise Airplanes* (Washington, DC: NASA Contractor Report 181817, July 1989); Boeing Commercial Airplane Company, *Application of Laminar Flow Control to Supersonic Transport Configurations* (Washington, DC: NASA Contractor Report 181917, July 1990).

94 NASA flight-test participants were: Dana Purifoy and Mark P. Stucky, research pilots; Marta R. Bohn-Meyer and Carol A. Reukauf, project managers; Michael P. Harlow, aircraft crew chief; Lisa J. Bjarke, DFRC principal investigator; and Michael C. Fischer, LaRC principal investigator.

95 See document number 6 at the end of this monograph for the flight log of the F-16XL number 2.

Status of Laminar-Flow Control Technology in the Mid-1990s

The status of laminar-flow control technology in the mid-1990s may be summarized as follows:

- Design methodology and related enabling technologies are far advanced beyond the X-21 levels.
- Improved manufacturing capabilities now permit the general aviation industry to incorporate natural laminar flow in some of its aircraft designs for chord length Reynolds numbers less than 20 million, but active laminar-flow control, required for larger aircraft and/ or aircraft with highly-swept wings, has not yet been applied to any operational aircraft.
- Although some additional structural and aerodynamic developments are required, the recent programs have brought the promise of laminar flow for moderately large and very large subsonic transport aircraft much closer to fruition than ever before.
- Hybrid laminar-flow control simplifies structure and systems and offers potential for 10- to 20-percent improvement in fuel consumption for moderate-size subsonic aircraft.
- Hybrid LFC may be the first application of suction-type laminar-flow control technology to large high-subsonic-speed transports because of its less risky nature.
- Although much of what has been learned about subsonic laminar-flow control is applicable to supersonic speeds, considerable additional work is required before supersonic laminar-flow control can be applied to operational aircraft.

Glossary

AACB   Aeronautics and Astronautics Coordinating Board

ACEE   Aircraft Energy Efficiency Program

AGARD   Advisory Group for Aeronautical Research & Development, North Atlantic Treaty Organization

AIAA   American Institute of Aeronautics and Astronautics

Attachment line   On a sweptback wing, the line at which the airflow divides to the upper and lower surfaces

Chord   The length of the surface from the leading to the trailing edge of an airfoil

DAG   Division Advisory Group

DFRC   Dryden Flight Research Center

DOD   Department of Defense

DOT   Department of Transportation

FAA   Federal Aviation Administration

GASP   Global Atmospheric Sampling Program

Glove   A special section of an airplane's lifting surface, usually overlaying the basic wing structure, that is designed specifically for research purposes

Hall   Originator of a theory that indicates when laminar flow would be lost as a function of atmospheric particle size and concentration

HLFC   Hybrid Laminar-Flow Control

Krueger flap   A specific type of leading-edge high-lift device (flap) that retracts into the wing lower surface. When used for an active laminar-flow control application, the flap also shields the wing from insect impacts during takeoff and landing and when retracted under the leading edge for cruise, does not interfere with the upper-surface laminar flow.

LaRC   Langley Research Center

LEFT   Leading-Edge Flight Test

Length Reynolds number   When the representative length in the formulation of the Reynolds number is chosen as the distance from the body's leading edge to the end of laminar flow, the resultant length Reynolds number can be used as a measure of the length of laminar flow attained.

LeRC	Lewis Research Center (now Glenn Research Center)
LFC	Laminar-flow control
LTPT	[Langley] Low-Turbulence Pressure Tunnel
NACA	National Advisory Committee for Aeronautics
NASA	National Aeronautics and Space Administration
NLF	Natural laminar flow
OAST	Office of Aeronautics and Space Technology of NASA
RAE	Royal Aircraft Establishment
Reynolds Number	A non-dimensional value equal to the product of the velocity of a body passing through a fluid, the density of the fluid, and a representative length divided by the fluid viscosity.
Three-dimensional type surface disturbances	Three-dimensional type surface disturbances are those with width or diameter to height ratios near a value of one.
Two-dimensional type disturbances	Examples of two-dimensional type disturbances are stream turbulence, noise, and surface irregularities having large ratios of width (perpendicular to the stream flow direction) to height, like spanwise surface steps due to mismatches in structural panels.
TACT	Transonic Aircraft Technology
Tollmien-Schlichting instabilities	Very small two-dimensional type disturbances that may induce transition to turbulent flow—named after German aerodynamicists Walter Tollmien and Hermann Schlichting.
USAF	United States Air Force
WADD	Wright Air Development Division

Documents

AERONAUTICS PANEL, AACB,

R&D REVIEW

REPORT OF THE SUBPANEL ON

AERONAUTICAL ENERGY CONSERVATION/FUELS

DECEMBER 5, 1974

Revised

Document 1—Aeronautics Panel, AACB, R&D Review, Report of the Subpanel on Aeronautical Energy Conservation/Fuels

4.1 Aerodynamics

4.1.1 Form and Induced Drag

The recommended program concerns the development of new wing concepts and configurations that offer potential for fuel conservation by reducing wing form and induced drag. Specifically, research on induced drag reduction concepts should exploit the relaxed restraints on wing geometry which are possible through the applications of advanced materials, active controls and advanced airfoils. Higher aspect ratios and lower wing sweep than currently used in existing aircraft are two areas where significant gains in the reduction of form and induced drag may be achieved. In order to realize these benefits, wind tunnel research must be done to optimize wing planforms. Also included in the program are studies to develop high design lift coefficient supercritical airfoils, necessary for suppression of transonic drag rise of high aspect ratio wings.

Studies of winglets at the Langley Research Center by Dr. R. T. Whitcomb are sufficiently promising to encourage increased effort. This fuel conserving concept has the attractive feature that it seems possible to retrofit existing aircraft with winglets, and thereby effect a near-term introduction of a fuel conserving concept into commercial and military service. Continued wind tunnel development of this concept is needed, and studies should now be undertaken to address the practical aspects of using winglets (e.g. - evaluations of structural weights, assessments of flutter problems, and comparisons with increased aspect ratio). Pending the outcome of these practicality studies, an existing aircraft should be fitted with winglets and flight tested to verify the performance gains. Consideration should be given to a joint USAF/NASA flight program with a military transport such as a KC-135.

4.1.2 Skin Friction

Although much of the required basic work in laminar flow control has been done, some aerodynamic research is needed to evaluate the effectiveness of now available lightweight porous or perforated composite materials as suction surfaces and to examine the application of LFC on supercritical airfoil sections. However, the primary need now is to bridge the gap between the aerodynamic experiments that have been done and the manufacturing and operational data needed for commercial or military transport design. This will require structural evaluations of LFC concepts to assure satisfactory performance of suction panels to meet the design criteria of transport aircraft and total systems integration studies to address the details of LFC component matching, suction surfaces, ducts, and suction compressors. Finally, a flight program will be required. This program will supply manufacturing data and experience, maintenance data, and operational experience essential to implementation of this energy-saving concept by the airframe manufacturers. A funding level for this flight program, beginning in the late 1970's, is anticipated to be approximately 60 million dollars.

Research on compliant walls is needed to uncover the mechanisms involved in the drag reduction phenomenon. Compliant materials should be studied to determine the properties which are important to achieve drag reduction and establish criteria to assure sound applications of compliant materials to aircraft. As the R&T efforts on compliant walls proceed, limited flight testing of the most promising materials could begin. Small panels of compliant materials would be fitted to aircraft in order to evaluate the durability of the materials in the flight environment. With the selection of the most promising material, a large panel would then be fitted to the fuselage of an existing aircraft and local skin friction reductions verified with in-flight measurements.

A small effort is included in the proposed program to continue R&T on air injection through slots as a means of reducing turbulent friction. Studies will be made to establish the effectiveness of this concept at low speeds.

4.1.3 Propulsion-Airframe Integration

The propulsion integration research is directed toward the reduction of aerodynamic drag and the development of favorable interference lift by proper integration of the propulsion system with the airframe. Fuel conserving concepts to be investigated would include the use of over-the-wing jet-blowing to reduce the induced drag; airframe, nacelle, and pylon contouring in reduce installation drag; and the use of thrust vectoring with supercirculation to improve cruise lift-drag ratios.

As indicated in the "Technical Opportunities" Section, propulsion integration studies are generally inhibited by a lack of capability in our wind tunnel facilities to adequately simulate Reynolds number. Therefore, this panel endorses the construction of high Reynolds number facilities to meet this need.

4.1.4 Aerodynamics of Controls

To achieve maximum benefits from the applications of active controls to commercial and military transports, more information is needed on the optimization of control surfaces on supercritical wings. These control surfaces could include leading and trailing edge controls, upper and lower surface spoilers, and other innovative concepts cuch as tip-mounted surfaces. Force and both steady and unsteady pressure measurements would be made on wind tunnel models to define chordwise and spanwise load distributions, hinge-moments, and control surface rate and amplitude requirements.

4.1.5 Unconventional Aircraft Configurations

Aerodynamic studies are needed to support development of unconventional aircraft concepts which can lead to significant energy conservation. Span loader concepts, for example, require the development of suitable thick airfoils; optimum airfoil contours for thickness ratios exceeding 20 percent must be determined.

The skewed wing concept has indicated in early tests that high cruise efficiency can be achieved over the Mach number range from 0.7 to 1.4. Further study is required to develop optimized skewed wing designs, evaluate aeroelastic behavior, and propulsion integration effects. In FY 1977, flight tests for a manned aircraft modified to accommodate an oblique wing is proposed.

4.1 AERODYNAMICS
(NASA)

PROGRAM AREA	DEFICIENCY/OPPORTUNITY	PROPOSED PROGRAM ADDITION	ADDITIONAL REQ'D FNDS NET R&D + RPM ($K) FY	
			76	77
FORM & INDUCED	• INDUCED DRAG REDUCTION WITH VORTEX DIFFUSERS (WINGLETS) (POSSIBLE RETROFIT)	• AERODYNAMIC EVALUATIONS	500	200
		• ANALYSIS OF PRACTICALITY (I.E. - WEIGHT, FLUTTER, COMPARISON WITH INCREASED AR)		
		• FLIGHT VALIDATION	1700	1000
	• TRANSONIC DRAG-RISE REDUCTION WITH SUPER-CRITICAL AERO	• STUDY HIGH DESIGN C_L AIRFOILS	250	250
		• STUDY WING DESIGNS, CONFIG. (HIGHER AR, LOWER SWEEP)		
		• LFC AERODYNAMIC STUDIES (SUPERCRITICAL AIRFOILS, SHOCKS, NOISE)		
SKIN-FRICTION	• MAINTENANCE OF LAMINAR FLOW WITH LAMINAR FLOW CONTROL	• MATERIALS FOR SUCTION SURFACES	750	800
		• STUDY LFC A/C SYSTEMS		
		• FLIGHT PROGRAM	(FUTURE)	60,000

43

PROGRAM AREA	DEFICIENCY/OPPORTUNITY	PROPOSED PROGRAM ADDITION	ADDITIONAL REQ'D FNL NET R&D + RPM ($K) FY	
			76	77
SKIN FRICTION	● TURBULENT FRICTION REDUCTION WITH COMPLIANT WALLS	● STUDY BASICS OF COMPLIANT WALL PHENOMENON ● DEVELOP COMPLIANT MATERIALS ● FLIGHT VALIDATE	450 / 0	450 / 500
	● TURBULENT FRICTION REDUCTION WITH AIR INJECTION	● ESTABLISH SUBSONIC EFFECTIVENESS	100	100
PROPULSION-AIRFRAME INTEGRATION	● SUPERCIRCULATION TO IMPROVED CRUISE L/D. (OVER-THE-WING BLOWING, THRUST VECTORING)	● WIND-TUNNEL STUDIES TO ESTABLISH EFFECTIVENESS	300	400
	● LACK OF SUFFICIENT RN IN FACILITIES	● SUPPORT CONSTRUCTION OF HIGH RN FACILITY		
AERODYNAMICS OF CONTROLS	● TRIM DRAG & WEIGHT REDUCTION WITH ACTIVE CONTROLS (REDUCED STABILITY MANEUVER AND GUST LOAD ALLEVIATION)	● ESTABLISH AERO DATA BASE ON THE EFFECTIVENESS OF CONTROLS (STATIC & DYNAMIC)	200	300

PROGRAM AREA	DEFICIENCY/OPPORTUNITY	PROPOSED PROGRAM ADDITION	ADDITIONAL REQ'D FNDS NET R&D + RPM ($K) FY	
			76	77
UNCONVENTIONAL A/C CONFIGURATIONS	• LARGE DEDICATED CARGO A/C (E.G., SPANLOADERS, TANDEM WING, TIPCOUPLED, ETC.)	• DEVELOP THICK AEROFOILS, AND 3D CONFIG.	300	600
	• SKEWED WING	• DEVELOP WING PLANFORMS, THICKNESS DISTRIBUTION, AND AIRFOIL SECTIONS FOR BEST EFFICIENCY	300	500
		• TEST AEROELASTIC MODELS		
		• EVALUATE PROPULSION INSTALLATION EFFECTS		
		• FLIGHT EVALUATIONS RPV, AND MANNED	500	2500

AERONAUTICAL SYSTEMS DIVISION

REPORT OF REVIEW GROUP ON

X-21A LAMINAR FLOW CONTROL PROGRAM

14-15 October 1965

at

NORAIR DIVISION, NORTHROP CORP.

HAWTHORNE, CALIFORNIA

8 November 1965

Document 2—Report of Review Group on X-21A Laminar Flow Control Program

I. INTRODUCTION AND HISTORICAL REVIEW:

A. The X-21A Laminar Flow Control Demonstration Program was initiated in August, 1960, following thorough studies and a recommendation by the Scientific Advisory Board Aerospace Vehicles Panel. With the predictable and repeatable attainment in flight of large laminar areas at high chord Reynolds numbers, the program has now reached a crucial stage. The proof of full operational practicability under field conditions emerges as a final, essential objective yet to be accomplished. If successful, such a demonstration would complete much of the groundwork necessary for applying LFC to a suitable military prototype.

B. The detailed progress of the X-21A program is well documented and need not be described here. By way of background, reference is made to the SAB Report of the Aerospace Vehicles Panel on "Boundary Layer Control", 25 June 1959. The program was reexamined by the Vehicles Panel in reports dated November 1961 and November 1962. More recently, the ASD Division Advisory Group held and reported on an extensive review of 22-23 June 1964, and there was a USAF Program Review on 13 January 1965.

C. As a follow-up step to the two reviews cited above, the need for the present review was reiterated in a letter, dated 17 September 1965, from Commander, Research and Technology Division, AFSC. The intention had been to assemble the original committee of last year which was composed of several individuals from the DAG and SAB plus representatives of the airframe industry, NASA and FAA. Because only one DAG member could attend, it was agreed to include non-DAG participants in the executive sessions and as signatories of this document, which fact explains why it cannot be formally identified as a DAC report. The chairman expresses his appreciation for the able participation and support of all industry, NASA and FAA representatives, as well as to the many Norair Division personnel for an efficient, responsive presentation.

D. The reviewing committee finds that most, but not all, of the technical recommendations made in the June 1964 report have been thoroughly implemented. The requirement for further flight research of a fundamental scientific nature is, however, regarded as secondary in comparison with the early accumulation of field operational experience on the X-21A. This conclusion is elaborated in Section II below. As expeditiously as possible the remainder of the program must be so oriented as to maximize its technological and operational contributions toward potential development of a military prototype embodying LFC. Although a number of questions are yet to be answered, the committee discussed and was favorably impressed by such concepts as laminarizing portions of the wing of a large military transport (e.g., one or two drawn from the C-5A line). The committee recommends that USAF intensify its study of such applications and ascertain the merits of LFC — relative to or in combination with reduced-SFC engines, hydrogen fuel, etc. — as a means for increasing range, endurance and/or payload.

II. CONCLUSIONS AND RECOMMENDATIONS:

The committee's conclusions are organized as responses to the five questions contained in the chartering letter. For completeness, these questions are also reproduced here.

A. ("What is the significance of results achieved during the past year?") A number of definite results have been obtained in the areas of

2

48

aerodynamics, structures and environmental influences. In a broad way, it can be said that distinct progress has been made and that a number of questions and problems which existed last year now have fairly clear answers. The results derived from work on these questions and problems will be enumerated and discussed.

i. _Aerodynamics._ Save for some uncertanties regarding leading-edge contamination by turbulence from the fuselage, the committee concludes that tests have verified the method of aerodynamic design. The basis for this statement is that the design remains as originally laid down several years ago, except for the leading-edge modifications. In mid-1964 it was believed that the cause of the trouble with the leading edge had been found. The resulting theory appears to have been confirmed, and design criteria to avoid the difficulty have been established.

Means for controlling leading-edge contamination from the fuselage have been developed and proven in flight. They are two in number: a special fence and a suction leading-edge portion containing vertical slots.

On some parts of the wing laminar runs up to length Reynolds number 46 million have been demonstrated. Last year consistently obtained maxima were less than half this figure. General research and engineering work have progressed to the point where aerodynamic design procedures suitable for Reynolds numbers of 60 million are known. They would, however, require flight verification.

Some direct over-all drag measurements by speed-power procedures have been made, resulting in good agreement with predictions. Slot design, with regard to size, has been placed on a more quantitative basis by means of a Reynolds number criterion determined from laboratory tests.

3

ii. <u>Structural Surface Criteria.</u> Knowledge has been gained concerning two aspects of the laminarized wing surface:

    1. A previously suggested criterion for the allowable size of single surface waves has been confirmed in flight.

    2. Vibration of isolated panels at a discrete frequency has not distrubed the laminar flow.

Although the maximum permissible waviness has not been established, the present requirements can be met using careful manufacturing techniques. The vibration and acoustic tests indicate that noise transmitted through the structure or local panel resonances will probably not be a problem for LFC airplanes.

iii. <u>Environment.</u> Appreciable new information has been gained concerning the effects of local environment on the functioning of the laminarized wing:

    1. <u>External noise:</u> Laminar flow persisted to sound levels approximately 6 db above the established criterion. The maximum allowable level was not determined, but further tests are proposed using an acoustic generator in the upper fuselage.

    2. <u>Internal noise:</u> Noise generated within the LFC suction ducts does not disturb the laminar flow unless the duct is forced at resonant frequencies that produce unusually large disturbances outside the suction slots.

    3. <u>Clouds:</u> Although laminarity is lost during flight through clouds, it is reestablished a few seconds after return to clear air.

    4. <u>Turbulence:</u> Atmospheric turbulence of a level to change the wing angle of attack through $\pm 1^\circ$ and to produce $\pm 0.3g$ of C.G. acceleration does not disturb the laminar flow.

4

5. <u>Off-design Flight</u>: Small alterations in flight condition ($\Delta c_L \simeq$ 0.04 or $\Delta M \simeq$ 0.03), resulting from maneuvers or changes in speed or altitude, have not affected the laminar flow to an appreciable extent.

6. <u>Insect Contamination</u>: Surface contamination due to insect strikes has not disturbed the laminar flow. However, the flights have been made in a desert area where the insect population is notably sparse and of small size. The favorable results so far are not necessarily indicative of the effects of world-wide operation.

B. ("What technical and operational considerations are as yet unanswered?") The conclusion was reached many years ago, based on extensive analysis and wind-tunnel studies on smooth models under carefully controlled conditions, that large areas of laminar flow could be maintained at high Reynolds numbers by means of boundary layer control. On the basis of these and subsequent investigations, the technical approach to aerodynamically designing an LFC wing has become reasonably well understood, although detailed design of a particular application will continue to require specific wind tunnel tests.

The primary questions which have not been completely answered through the years relate to the practical aspects of applying LFC to a full-scale airplane. They may be itemized more specifically as follows:

i. Can the structure be designed and fabricated in such a way that the surfaces comply with the stringent criteria on roughness and waviness? What are the weight and complexity of the structure?

ii. If such a structure can be manufactured, to what extent does the surface deteriorate under operational conditions?

5

iii. What are the difficulties involved in maintaining the wing in a sufficiently smooth condition to ensure the attainment of extensive laminar flow on a routine basis? The problems of keeping the surface free from such disturbances as insects, mud, rain, etc., are implied here.

iv. What tolerance does laminar flow have to such in-flight environmental factors as rain, sleet, ice crystals, clouds and gustiness?

v. What are the effects of maneuvering flight, off-design lift coefficient and non-optimum suction distribution?

The X-21A was developed to answer these operational questions. Up to this time the program has not been able completely to address itself to them, because of difficulties involved with the basic aerodynamic design. These difficulties have been overcome. The committee concludes that the program should now be directed toward answering these questions.

It is recommended that, during the proposed operational phase employing the X-21A with a re-surfaced wing, specific attention be directed toward the following considerations:

i. Maintainability and reliability factors of LFC should be collected to USAF standard procedures and requirements, so that a quantitative comparison can be made to current non-LFC availability.

ii. Maintenance personnel should be trained, procedures should be developed and data accumulated in a statistical form useful for assessing the incremental penalty for incorporating LFC in transport type aircraft in service.

iii. Simulated or real missions should be conducted with as much validity to ZI and world-wide MATS operations as program funding and test aircraft capability permit.

6

iv. Historical records of LFC material failures and maintenance activity should be kept and reduced to information useful for future detailed design.

v. Realistic penalties of LFC should be determined, in regard to weather and environmental factors for basing, ground protection, flight profile and other flight performance factors.

C. ("What future development effort is considered necessary and/or desirable?") The attainment of an operational suitability evaluation is the minimum development effort that is absolutely necessary in order to justify any commitment of further funds on the X-21A program.

The program extension should necessarily be focused on supporting a modification to the wing that AFFTC believes will be adequate for obtaining credible operational and maintenance data. The time estimates presented in the Continuation Schedules listed by the Norair briefing as Alternates I, II, and III are much too relaxed, and costs could also be reduced by an accelerated effort.

It is desirable that the operational evaluation tests to be run by AFFTC have full coordination with both MATS and the Airlift Panel of the Air Staff, so as to increase the acceptability of the procedures and hence the results. During the evaluation of the flight test data, an airframe manufacturing company, an airline operator and FAA should be asked to review and prepare evaluation reports.

It is necessary that sufficient funds be included in the terminal expenditures to document the design, operational and maintenance data in a form usable by other airframe manufacturers.

7

It is recommended that continuing support be given to work on the state of the art of LFC. The continued pursuit of research and exploratory development in this field should not be entirely contingent on the X-21A program, so that an ultimate separation of USAF funding for these two types of activity seems desirable. Exploratory development funds appear to be the logical channel for support.

D. ("Has the need for the major modification been justified?") It was a consensus of the committee that the need for some sort of major modification to the X-21A wings, with the primary purpose of providing a vehicle suitable for realistic operational testing, has been justified. To assure timeliness, the modified aircraft should be turned over to AFFTC well in advance of dates given in the Norair LFC Continuation Schedule. Although the partial modification proposed by Norair is possibly satisfactory, serious consideration must be given to building a wholly new set of metal upper wing surfaces needing no application of filler to meet aerodynamic smoothness criteria. The committee was informed that this alternative implies no large percentage increase in the program cost.

The third alternative of immediately closing out the flight program is particularly undesirable at present, in view of current consideration being given to the development of a prototype large military transport with LFC. Especially in the operational area, the data to be generated with the modified vehicle are regarded as essential for supporting the PDP prerequisites for concept formulation on any new LFC vehicle.

The scheme of simulating an entire wing by means of a fraction of the total X-21A wing area, for purposes of the operational evaluation, is deemed barely adequate rather than optimum. Whatever the modification, however,

8

the committee understands that AFFTC has given assurance that a full test program can be conducted as soon as an acceptable vehicle is available.

E. ("How should the program be brought to a satisfactory conclusion?") In line with the foregoing recommendations, the program should be brought to a conclusion by an expeditious flight operational demonstration, as well as by the simultaneous collection and correlation of results and information to facilitate direct application to the design of projected aircraft.

The resulting data should be in such form that they are of immediate value to designers. Procedures should be included for determining suction distribution; slot size, location and spacing; duct size and matching; pumping requirements; tolerance limits and the manufacturing and maintenance technology relevant to these limits. Additionally the operational limits of speed, altitude, Reynolds number, weather and other environmental factors should be established.

F. Beyond the various points brought out in the above replies, one other area seemed to the committee to deserve expanded activity. Since considerable progress has been made in the development of design techniques, especially of an aerodynamic nature, it is now important to determine, through a thorough and definitive systems analysis and on a cost-effectiveness basis, the potential payoff of LFC application for range, endurance and payload increases. Such studies would provide a basis for assessing the value of LFC and furnish comparisons with other possible technical approaches to such extended performance. Competitive technologies exist, for example, in improved SFC engines, lighter-weight structural materials, hydrogen fuel and even refueling systems.

It must also be realized that operational missions might be extended to a

9

dramatic degree by using LFC in combination with these other technologies, since they are not incompatible with it.

As already noted, there still remain pieces of data that are not fully developed but are essential for consideration in any effectiveness study. Unit maintenance costs, operational costs and structural weight penalties are illustrations. Nevertheless, the committee believes that sophisticated systems analyses can be undertaken in a timely fashion and that results of the extended X-21A program can be phased in so as to provide credible conclusions.

Technically it is feasible to consider partial laminarization of wing, tail and/or body surfaces, so as to assess those areas with their increased construction costs, etc., in comparison with full laminarization of aerodynamic surfaces. The idea is to establish cost effectiveness tradeoffs in terms of percentage of laminarized area, as contrasted with an optimized turbulent-flow aircraft.

To achieve the greatest practical value, it is important that either an existing heavy cargo aircraft or one whose development is firmly committed serve as a base point for the recommended analyses. In making cost comparisons, this design should then be modified into an optimized aerodynamic, structural and propulsive configuration for LFC application.

Prepared by:

Prof. Holt Ashley, SAB & DAG (Chairman)
Mr. W.H. Hannon, Lockheed
Mr. Harold D. Hoekstra, FAA
Mr. Laurence K. Loftin, NASA
Prof. B.H. Larsohner, Colorado State University
Mr. Verlin Reed, NASA
Mr. Leonard M. Rose, North American Aviation
Mr. A.M.O. Smith, Douglas Aircraft Co.
Mr. John K. Wimpress, The Boeing Co.

10

SUBJECT: X-21, Laminar Flow Control Program

TO: Members of Review Group

1. We have reached a point in time and place where some major decisions must be made regarding the future of the X-21 Laminar Flow Control Demonstration Program. Toward this end, a program review has been organized under the auspices of the ASD Division Advisory Group, to take place on 14-15 October 1965 at the Norair Division of the Northrop Corporation, Hawthorne, California. I would greatly appreciate your participation in this review and your recommendations as to the future conduct of this program.

2. This review is a follow-on to the program review conducted in June 1964 which resulted in several recommendations for additional investigation, testing, and instrumentation prior to a commitment to proceed with a major modification of the wing. The recommended program of work has been completed and the following questions must now be addressed:

    a. What is the significance of results achieved during the past year?

    b. What technical and operational considerations are as yet unanswered?

    c. What future development effort is considered necessary and/or desirable?

    d. Has the need for the major modification been justified?

    e. How should the program be brought to a satisfactory conclusion?

3. Your acceptance of this invitation to participate would be most gratifying.

M.C. DEMLER
Major General, USAF
Commander

11

X-21 TECHNICAL REVIEW AGENDA
14-15 Oct 1965

Beginning at 0830, Thursday, 14 Oct 1965
Northrop Aircraft Corporation
3901 W. Broadway
Hawthorne, California
(Transportation will be furnished from the
Ramada Inn, 9620 Airport Blvd., Los Angeles)

A. Summary of Previous Reviews

B. Norair Presentations

    1. Flight Results

        a. Laminar Areas (Repeatability, Turbulent Spot Investigations,
            Slot Velocity Measurements, Instrumentation, Leading Edge
            Contamination and Fixes)

        b. Length Reynolds Number

        c. Performance and Drag Analysis

    2. Wind Tunnel Results (Norair and Ames)

    3. Acoustics and Vibration Results (Flight Test, Norair and Ames
        Wind Tunnels, Laboratory Duct Model, Panel Vibration Test)

    4. Correlation of Theoretical and Experimental Data, Design Criteria,
        Suction Distributions, Tolerances

    5. Operational Considerations

        a. Maintenance, Waviness, Surface Roughness, Cleaning

        b. Weather and Insects

    6. Applicability of Data to Future Aircraft

    7. Recommended Follow-on Program Alternates

C. Review Group Discussion

D. DAG Recommendations (Closed Session)

12

X-21 DAG REVIEW

14 October 1965

4th Floor Conference Room

<u>AGENDA</u>   14 October 1965

8:00 a.m.   Bus Departs Ramada Inn for Northrop Norair

8:20 a.m.   Arrive Engineering Science Center Lobby

9:00 a.m.   Welcoming Remarks - R. E. Horner

9:10 a.m.   Purposes of the Review - MajGen M. C. Demler

9:20 a.m.   Program Highlights and Cost Summary - T. H. Goss

9:30 a.m.   Review of Previous DAG Recommendations - P. Antonatos

9:40 a.m.   Break

10:00 a.m.   Introduction and Summary of Northrop Presentation -
                Dr. L. R. Fowell

10:45 a.m.   Wind Tunnel Investigations - Dr. W. Pfenninger

11:30 a.m.   Acoustics and Vibration Tests - G. L. Gluyas

11:50 a.m.   Performance Tests (Drag) - G. L. Gluyas

12:00   Lunch - Norair Cafeteria

1:00 p.m.   Configuration Development and Correlation of Flight
                Test Results with Criteria - R. K. Bucher

2:00 p.m.   Applicability of Data to Future Aircraft - S. H. Brown

2:15 p.m.   Recommended Continuation Program - R. W. Bratt

2:45 p.m.   Break

3:00 p.m.   Open Discussions

5:00 p.m.   Bus Departs Northrop Norair for Ramada Inn

                            15 October 1965

8:30 a.m.   Bus Departs Ramada Inn for Northrop Norair

X-21 DAG REVIEW

ATTENDEES

VISITORS

✓ Holt Ashley, MIT - Chairman
✓ Major General M. C. Demler, RTD
Lieutenant Colonel Louis R. Sert, RTD
Captain Wyatt, RTD
Phil P. Antonatos, RTD
Joe Nenni, RTD, AFFDL
✓ F. D. Orazio, RTD, Systems Engineering Group
✓ A. Braslow, NASA
✓ L. K. Loftin, NASA
✓ J. B. Parkinson, NASA
✓ Verlin Reed, NASA
Dr. B. H. Goethert, AFSC
Major Carey, AFSC
Major Lewis, AFSC
✓ J. K. Wimpress, Boeing
J. McCollom, ASD
Ted Goss, ASD
Captain Cassler, ASD
✓ B. H. Marshner, Colorado State University
✓ L. N. Rose, North American Aviation
✓ H. Hoekstra, FAA - Washington
~~R. H. Widmer, General Dynamics~~
~~R. Smelt, Lockheed~~
✓ A. M. O. Smith, Douglas
Captain Peterson, AFFTC, Edwards AFB
Major W. Ennis, Edwards AFB
R. Sudderth, Edwards AFB
✓ W. H. Hannan, Lockheed
Colonel R. K. Keeling, AFPRO
Captain J. S. Ford, AFPRO

NORAIR

R. E. Horner	R. C. Whites
W. E. Gasich	R. R. Wingert
M. Kuska	J. C. Carlson
L. R. Fowell	J. S. Bacon
W. Pfenninger	R. Thompson
R. W. Bratt	R. F. Carmichael
G. L. Gluyas	J. W. Quick
R. K. Bucher	R. C. Clemens
W. G. Wheldon	O. A. Levi
S. H. Brown	W. Bailey
R. E. Kosin	

LANGLEY RESEARCH CENTER
ANNOUNCEMENT

NUMBER
93-75

DATE
Sept. 12, 1975

SDL NUMBER(s)
032

SUBJECT: Establishment of Laminar Flow Control Working Group

The Langley Research Center has accepted the responsibility of implementing a research and technology program focused on the development and demonstration of economically feasible, reliable, and maintainable laminar flow control systems for viscous drag reduction. A three-phase program is envisioned: (1) development of practical materials, structural, suction, and aerodynamic concepts; (2) system development including design, fabrication, and ground or flight tests of system components; and (3) pending favorable results in the first two phases, a flight-test validation of laminar flow control (LFC) on a transport airplane.

A Laminar Flow Control (LFC) Working Group is hereby established to define a program of required R&T activities, appraise progress, and recommend program changes or additions. Working group members will serve as points of contact for each division involved in the program, and will devote such time as necessary to meet the program objectives. The group will functionally report to the Chief, Aeronautical Systems Division, and general program plans shall be concurred with by the Directors for Aeronautics, Electronics, Structures, and Systems Engineering and Operations.

Members of the LFC Working Group are designated as follows:

A. L. Braslow, Chairman	Aeronautical Systems Division
T. F. Bonner, Jr.	Systems Engineering Division
E. Boxer	Aeronautical Systems Division
D. M. Bushnell	High-Speed Aerodynamics Division
H. H. Heyson	Aeronautical Systems Division
M. M. Mikulas, Jr.	Structures and Dynamics Division
J. B. Peterson, Jr.	Subsonic Transonic Aerodynamics Division
R. A. Pride	Materials Division
L. W. Taylor, Jr.	Flight Dynamics and Control Division
R. T. Taylor	Flight Research Division
R. D. Wagner	Aeronautical Systems Division

Edgar M. Cortright
Director

cc: All Supervisory Personnel

ADDRESS LABEL SPACE

N-32

Document 3—Langley Research Center Announcement: Establishment of Laminar Flow Control Working Group

INTERCENTER AGREEMENT

FOR

LAMINAR FLOW CONTROL

LEADING EDGE GLOVE FLIGHTS

BETWEEN

LANGLEY RESEARCH CENTER AND DRYDEN FLIGHT RESEARCH CENTER

PREPARED BY:

Richard D. Wagner
Aircraft Energy Efficiency Project Office
NASA Langley Research Center

Robert S. Baron
Project Test Liaison Office
NASA Dryden Flight Research Center

APPROVED B:

Donald P. Hearth
Director
NASA Langley Research Center

DATE: 4-1-80

Isaac T. Gillam, IV
Director
NASA Dryden Flight Research

DATE: 4-29-80

Document 4—Intercenter Agreement for Laminar Flow Control Leading Edge Glove Flights, LaRC and DFRC

Introduction

The Laminar Flow Control (LFC) Element of the NASA Aircraft Energy Efficiency (ACEE) Program is concerned with the development and demonstration of a practical, reliable, and maintainable LFC system for application to future commercial transport aircraft. The objective of the LFC Leading Edge Flight Test (LEFT) is to demonstrate the effectiveness of LFC leading edge systems under representative flight conditions. Operable LFC leading edge systems (including suction, cleaning, and deicing systems) will be installed in segments of the leading edge of the NASA JetStar. Two such test articles will be provided by contractors and flight tested at Dryden.

Nature of Program

Contracts will be awarded to the Lockheed-Georgia Company and the Douglas Aircraft Company. Each will cover the design and fabrication of an LFC leading edge systems test article. The Lockheed-Georgia Company will have the added task to perform the lead role to design the aircraft modification necessary to incorporate both the test articles and provide adequate systems support. Dryden will modify the test aircraft to the Lockheed-Georgia design and install the flight test articles. Both contractors will provide engineering support during the aircraft modification, test article installations, and acceptance ground and flight testing as a riate. Initial contracts will terminate upon completion of acceptan light testing. A NASA flight research program will then be initiated and n contracts will be negotiated with the contractors for support of this research flight testing. The flight test program will consist of four parts:

(1) An LFC systems performance demonstration.
(2) A cleaning and deicing systems performance demonstration.
(3) A simulated airline service operations program.
(4) An LFC flight research program.

About 200 flight hours are planned for the first three p s above (50 for the performance demonstrations and 150 for the operations Program). The LFC flight research program has not been formulated at this time and would be contingent upon availability of funds.

Principal Responsibilities and Assignments

As lead center for the LFC Element of the NASA ACEE Project, Langley will:

(a) Be responsible for overall management of the project and the contracts with the Lockheed-Georgia Company and the Douglas Aircraft Company.

(b) Coordinate and conduct reviews of task assignment plans and the preliminary and detail designs.

(c) Establish flight test requirements to accomplish program objectives.

(d) Evaluate and concur on flight test plans.

(e) Provide technical support of the flight testing and assume the lead role in providing for analysis of flight data and reporting of results.

Dryden will:

(a) Approve all flight test plans.

(b) Be responsible for flight safety.

(c) Be responsible for flight testing with contractor engineering support for the operation and maintenance of LFC systems on board the test aircraft.

(d) Participate in the management and technical reviews of the contractor task assignment plans and the preliminary and detail designs.

(e) Provide approval on the aircraft modification design.

(f) Assess instrumentation and data acquisition requirements and provide, as available: flight test instrumentation; data recording and reduction systems; and data reduction support.

(g) Perform the aircraft modifications and test article installations.

(h) Design, fabricate, and install the instrumentation and control consoles for the test articles.

(i) Participate in data analysis and reporting of results.

Major Milestones

1.	Contract awards	July 1980
2.	Instrumentation selection	October 1980
3.	Control consoles layout	January 1981
4.	Control consoles fabrication	January 1982
5.	Modified A/C design	March 1982
6.	Flight test hardware delivery to DFRC by contractor	June 1982

7. A/C modification complete   November 1982

8. Acceptance flight test complete   February 1983

9. Research flight test complete   August 1984
    (parts 1, 2, & 3)

10. Flight Test reports   June 1983 &
                                    September 1984

Funding Amounts and Sources

Langley RTOP 534-01-13

	FY '80	FY '81	FY '82	FY '83	FY '84
Program R & D Funds	3000	4200	2140	170	150
Dryden R & D/IMS	75/60	500/135	200/165	170/150	150/120

Data Acquisition, Analysis, and Distribution

Both Langley and Dryden will be responsible for management, analysis, and reporting of all flight data. Reporting of program results will be through joint (Langley and Dryden) NASA publications on flight test results and contractor final reports to document all contractor tasks.

NF-111

FLIGHT REPORT

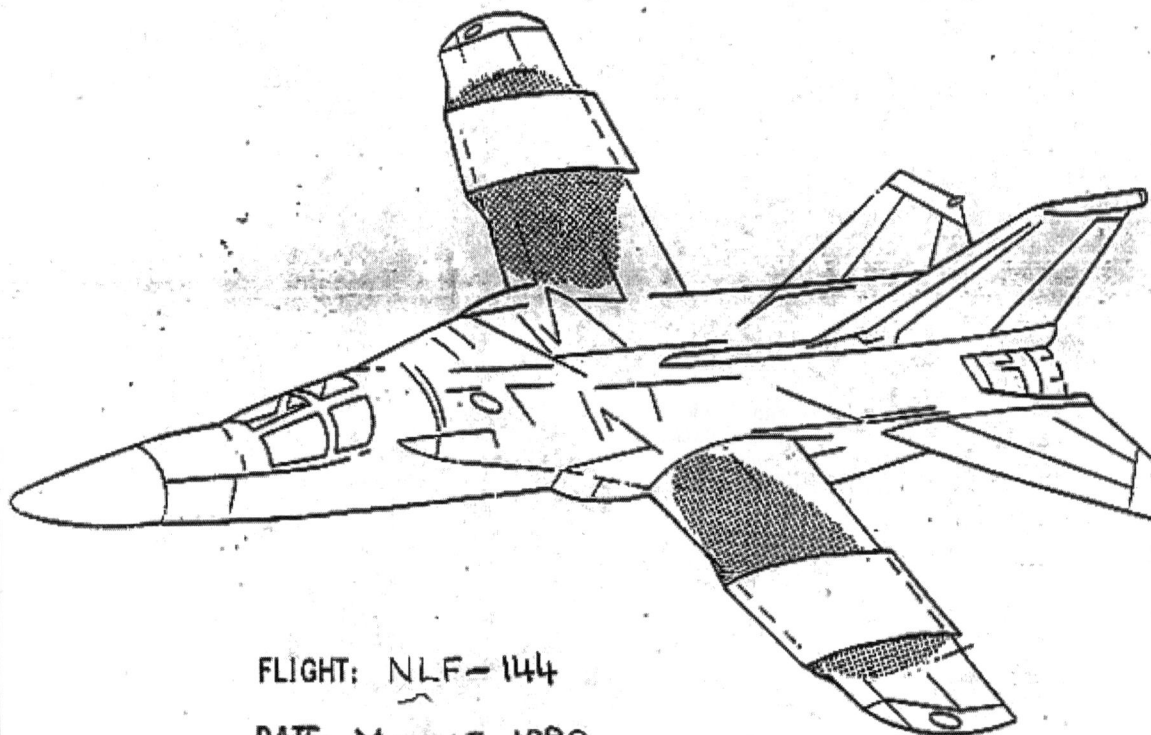

FLIGHT: NLF-144

DATE: May 15, 1980

Approved:

Lawrence J. Caw
NASA DFRC Project Manager

Louis L. Steers
NASA DFRC Project Engineer

Document 5—Flight Report, NLF-144, of AFTI/F-111 Aircraft with the TACT Wing Modified by a Natural Laminar Flow Glove

Pilot's notes and comments

Flight: 144   **Date:** 5/15/80

Flight 144 was the first flight of the AFTI-F-111 aircraft with the TACT wing modified by a Natural Laminar Flow (NFL) glove. The NLF modification necessitated flying the aircraft without spoilers and flaps. This resulted in degraded handling qualities, and longer takeoff and landing rolls than the unmodified aircraft.

The maximum power takeoff was accomplished at 16° leading edge wing sweep with the flight control system in "takeoff and land" and with ten thousand pounds fuel. The aircraft had a tendency to over-rotate as rotation was initiated at 170 KCAS. The rotation was stabilized at a nine degree pitch change from the pitch attitude prior to brake release. Moderate forward stick force was required to control angle of attack after lift-off. Takeoff trim had been set to 3.8° TEU. Elevator trim of 0° is suggested for the following flight. The takeoff handling qualities were judged satisfactory (calm wind).

The aircraft was cleaned up, the flight control system switch changed to normal, wings swept to 26°, and accelerated to 300 KCAS.

Several low approaches were then flown at 10° α with the gear down, flight control system in "takeoff and land," and wing at 26° sweep. The aircraft was judged to have a lateral PIO tendency throughout the landing approach. The full stop landing was accomplished with 4500 pounds of fuel. The lateral PIO tendency during this approach was amplified somewhat during the flare and touchdown. The outboard spoilers were enabled (in the ground roll mode) at touchdown, however, they were not sufficient to cause the aircraft to rest firmly on the gear during the aero-braking phase of the landing rollout. Without the stabilizing action due to squatting on the landing gear the lateral control during landing roll was rated acceptable (calm wind.) Brakes were applied at 110 KCAS with 3000 feet of runway remaining after a landing roll of about 11,000 feet. The landing roll was safely accomplished on the 15,000 foot runway.

Michael R. Swann
Aerospace Research Pilot

Project Pilot

Airplane Malfunction and Failures
Summary

Flight: 144   **Date:** 5/15/80

Flight number 144 was flown on 15 May 1980 in order to structurally verify and to evaluate the handling qualities of the NLF modification on the F-111A aircraft. The aircraft was fueled with a partial fuel load for a total of 12,000 lbs (10,500 lbs fwd; 1,500 lbs aft). Total flying time for the flight was 35 minutes.

In order to structurally verify the NLF modification, a check point at 10,000 ft, .55 Mach number, 305 knots at 26° wing sweep was accomplished. Following this test point, the aircraft performed several low approaches to runway 22 to evaluate the handling qualities.

Post flight inspection of the NLF modification revealed no anomalies. Small cracks did appear on the flap hinge line in the non test section of the NLF glove. This was expected due to previous experience with test samples.

Following the inspection of the NLF modification, a turnaround preflight was accomplished and the aircraft was refueled with a full fuel load and released for flight.

Operations Engineer

Instrumentation Post - Flight Summary

Flight: ___144___   **Date:** 5/15/80

This was a good data flight.

There were no encoding or recording problems noted on post-flight.

The series of flights starting with this flight have been instrumented for

1) Pressure distribution over NLF glove test section,
2) Boundary layer characteristics over NLF glove test section, and
3) Base pressure measurements on body of revolution on top of vertical fin for base drag experiment.

A schematic of these is shown in Figure F-1.

Item 1 involved the relocation of 34 existing TACT pressure orifices. A schematic showing NLF instrumentation is given in Figure F-1. The list of parmid's and location is given in Table F-1.

Item 2 involved the use of two identical 20 probe 5 inch rakes, Figure F-2. The top two probes are not hooked for this experiment. Table F-1 gives the parmid's for the probes.

Item 3 required a scanivalve to be installed in the body of revolution, Figure F-3a. The parmid's are given in Figure F-3b. Figure F-3c gives locations of the parmid's on the base.

Wilson E. VanDiver
Instrumentation Engineer

F-111 NATURAL LAMINAR FLOW (NLF) EXPERIMENT

BODY OF REVOLUTION BASE DRAG EXPERIMENT

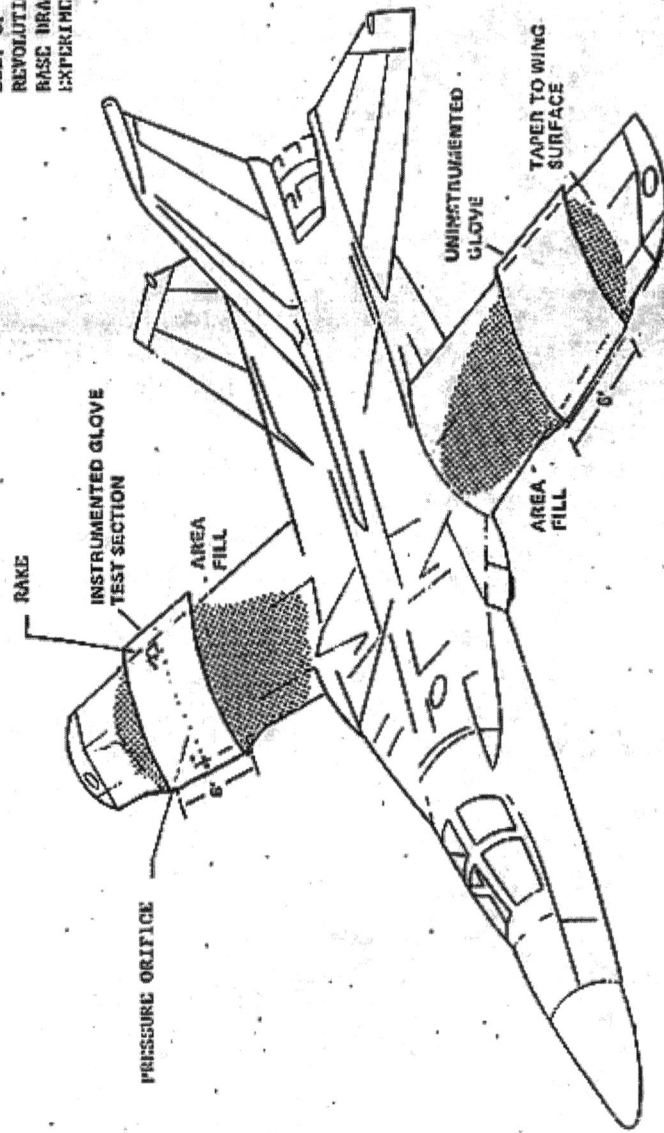

UNINSTRUMENTED GLOVE

TAPER TO WING SURFACE

AREA FILL

RAKE

INSTRUMENTED GLOVE TEST SECTION

AREA FILL

PRESSURE ORIFICE

Supersonic Laminar Flow Control Flight Record.lb

F-16XL Flt#	SLFC Flt#	Flt Date	Hrs this Flt	# Test Points	Pilot	Back Seat	Controller	Max. Alt	Objectives	Comments
44	1	10/13/95	1.1	5	Purifoy	Collard	Bohn Meyer	30K	FCF	
45	2	10/25/95	0.9	4	Purifoy	Collard	Bohn Meyer	50K	Loads clearance, Load/HQ evaluation, Air refuelling checks, Engine checks, Flutter clearance, PID, Performance	
46	3	11/8/95	1.35	15	Purifoy	Collard	Bohn Meyer	50K	Loads/HQ evaluation, Engine checks, In-flight refueling checks	
47	4	11/20/95	3.7	38	Purifoy	Collard	Bohn Meyer	40K	Loads clearance, Flutter clearance, Engine clearance	
48	5	1/24/96	2.6	7	Purifoy	Collard	Bohn Meyer	50K	Loads expansion, SLFC data	
49	6	1/26/96	1.8	26	Purifoy	Collard	Bohn Meyer	50K	T/C functional checks, Suction system evaluation, SLFC data	
									Loads clearance, TC performance and oil bypass, servo-on-mass-flow mode checks	
50	7	2/1/96	0.4	0	Purifoy	Collard	Bohn Meyer	50K	SLFC data at design Mach and altitude, TC start up procedure evaluation, servo-on-mass-flow mode evaluation	In-flight emergency due to left main landing gear door non-retract, RTB
51	8	2/2/96	2.5	20	Purifoy	Collard	Bohn Meyer	50K	SLFC data on leading edge, Evaluate River Run for flight operations	
52	9	2/9/96	2.6	19	Purifoy	Meyer	Bohn Meyer	50K	Servo-on-mass-flow mode evaluation, Use of hot films to determine existence of laminar flow, turbocompressor would not start	
53	10	2/15/96	1.2	0	Purifoy	Collard	Bohn Meyer	50K	of TC after SOV replacement, SLFC with hot films, communication problem	
54	11	2/22/96	1.6	4	Purifoy	Collard	Bohn Meyer	50K suction	between OSSC-C and downlink - no suction	

Document 6—Flight Record, F-16XL Supersonic Laminar Flow Control Aircraft

F-18/2 Flt	SLFC Flt	RT Date	Hrs Fls Flt	#Test Points	Pilot	Back Seat	Controller	Max Alt	Objectives	Comments
55	12	2/29/96	3.2	11	Purifoy	Stucky	Yamanaka	50K	...off; Begin checkout of second pilot, Recurrency training for backup controller; Validate OSSC system, Validate ATC communications	In-flight emergency due to right main gear door down
56	13	3/1/96	0.5	0	Stucky	Purifoy	Collard	50K	SLFC with suction system on and off	
57	14	3/6/96	2.1	19	Stucky	Purifoy	Collard	50K	Complete flight qualification of 2nd pilot, SLFC data with suction on/off, Red phone training for backup structures engineer	
58	15	3/8/96	2.3	14	Stucky	Meyer	Collard	50K	SLFC data with suction on	
59	16	3/15/96	2.4	34	Purifoy	Collard	Yamanaka	50K	SLFC data to determine minimum suction requirements on rooftop regions 14 & 15 and leading edge	
60	17	3/22/96	1.0	7	Stucky	Collard	Yamanaka	50K	SLFC data to document baseline shock fence configuration	TC experienced RPM overspeed with auto shutdown
61	18	4/17/96	3.1	50	Purifoy	Collard	Yamanaka	50K	Update loads envelope, SLFC data for no shock fence configuration, Determined minimum G limit for suction during pushover maneuvers	
62	19	4/23/96	1.4	16	Purifoy	Collard	Bohn Meyer	50K	Determine effectiveness of new larger shock fence	
63	20	4/25/96	3.1	49	Purifoy	Meyer	Bohn Meyer	50K	Complete evaluation of shock fence configuration	FCS caution light - but cleared
64	21	5/1/96	1.1	14	Purifoy	Bohn Meyer	Collard	50K	Define suction distribution with new shock fence	FCS caution - declared In-flight emergency

Flight Record.lb

Eject2 Flt#	SLFC Flt#	FLT Date	Hrs Obs/Br	# Test Points	Pilot	Back Seat	Controller	Max. Alt	Objectives	Comments
65	22	5/8/96	0.8	0		Collard	Yamanaka			FCS caution - declared in-flight emergency, First CHAGS flight, Had replaced ECA
66	23	5/8/96	0.8	14	Purifoy	Bohn Meyer	Yamanaka			FCS caution - declared in-flight emergency, Had replaced channel D power inverter
67	24	5/8/95	1.0	1	Purifoy	Collard	Yamanaka	55K	SLFC research data	
68	25	5/17/96	1.0	0	Purifoy	Collard	Yamanaka		FCS checkout, Loads clearance @ 55K,	FCS caution - declared in-flight emergency, AICS box was functional
69	26	5/29/96	0.9	16	Purifoy	Collard	Yamanaka	55K	FCS checkout, Loads clearance @ 45K, 42K, and 40K, SLFC data	
70	27	5/31/96	1.25	13	Purifoy	Meyer	Yamanaka	50K	SFLC data to obtain increased laminar flow	SLFC data, FCS caution declared in-flight emergency
71	28	6/7/96	3.1	31	Stucky	Collard	Yamanaka	5DK	SLFC data with lower surface masking (unsuccessful), Tufts and video	
72	29	6/12/96	2.0	15	Purifoy	Collard	Yamanaka	55K	SLFC data masking lower surface perforations (unsuccessful), Tufts, T/O delayed due to pyro inspection	
73	30	6/14/96	0.9	8	Stucky	Collard	Yamanaka	50K	SLFC suction level verification of extent of laminar flow	
74	31	6/28/96	3.0	21	Purifoy .	Meyer	Bohn Meyer	50K	SLFC data with filled turbulence diverter	
75	32	6/28/96	2.0	31	Purifoy	Meyer	Bohn Meyer	50K	SLFC data (unsuccessful)	

Flight Record.lb

F-16XL2 Flt#	SLFC Flt#	FLT Date	Hrs/flts Flt	# Test Points	Pilot	Back Seat	Controller	Max Alt	Objectives	Comments
76	33	7/8/96	2.0	24	Purifoy	Bohn Meyer	Yamanaka	53K	SLFC data with gap filled beneath shock fence, Varying alphas	
77	34	7/12/96	1.8	15	Purifoy	Collard	Yamanaka	53K	Investigate best suction levels at M2.0 with top of region 11 masked & det, turb wedge angle from H.F. on inbrd suction panel	
78	35	7/9/96	2.0	18	Purifoy	Collard	Yamanaka/ Wilcox	53K	Investigate best suction levels at M2.0 with top of region 11 masked	
79	36	7/13/96	3.0	31	Purifoy	Collard	Yamanaka/ Wilcox	53K	Investigate best suction levels at M2.0 with no masking, varying alpha and beta	
80	37	7/26/96	3.0	34	Purifoy	Collard	Yamanaka/ Wilcox	53K	Code Calibration data	
81	38	8/16/96	3	41	Purifoy	Bohn Meyer	Collard/ Wilcox	53K	Code Calibration data and baseline data for shock fence toe-in	
82	39	8/28/96	2.7	27	Purifoy	Collard	Yamanaka/ Wilcox	53K	Evaluate results of shock fence toe-in, checkout canopy ring mod technique	
83	40	9/3/96	3.2	13	Stucky	Collard	Yamanaka/ Wilcox	54K	Determine effectiveness of canopy fairing, get more info on turb wedge angle	
84	41	8/20/96	3.1	43	Purifoy	Collard	Yamanaka/ Wilcox	55K	Determine effectiveness of canopy fairing; get more info on turb wedge angle, rooftop suction reduction	
85	42	10/4/96	2.9	48	Purifoy	Collard	Wilcox	55K	Determine effectiveness of canopy fairing, obtain SLFC data for rooftop, leading edge, and uniform suction reduction	

Flight Record.lb

E-field2 Flt #	SLEE Flt #	FLT Date	Hrs/life Flt	# Test Points	Pilot	Back Seat	Controller	Max Alt	Objectives	Comments
86	45	11/26/96	2.7	43	Purifoy	Collard	Wilcox	53K	Using the 60° shock fence obtain data for code calibration and the inboard turbulent region. Also, obtain Anderson Current Loop data and Optical Sensor data.	
86	44	11/13/96	1.3	0	Purifoy	Collard	Wilcox	51K		FCS caution light for LE flap, RTB declaring IFE
85	43	10/24/96	3.2	48	Purifoy	Bohn Meyer	Collard	52K	Using the 60° shock fence obtain data the optimum flight conditions determined using the 60° fence. Also, obtain Anderson Current Loop data.	
			TOTALS:	90.6	796					

Index

American Institute of Aeronautics and Astronautics, 13

Department of Defense, 14

Department of Transportation, 14

Federal Aviation Administration, 10, 14

National Advisory Committee for Aeronautics,1, 3, 10, 15

National Aeronautics and Space Administration, 1, 10-11, 14, 28

Ames Research Center, 18

Dryden Flight Research Center, 8, 17, 20-29, 33

Langley Research Center, 3, 4, 10, 13, 15, 20-21, 31, 32-33

Lewis Research Center, 28

Office of Aeronautics and Space Technology, 14

National Bureau of Standards, 4

Royal Aircraft Establishment (Great Britain), 6, 8

U.S. Air Force, 5-6, 8, 10-12, 31

Wright Air Development Division, 10

Perforation method

electron beam, 24-25

laser, 25

Peterson, John B. Jr., 20

Pfenninger, Werner, 5, 8, 22

Prandtl, Ludwig, 1

Programs

Aircraft Energy Efficiency (ACEE), 14-16, 21-22, 26

Advanced Technology Transport, 13 n

Global Atmospheric Sampling Program, 28

Leading Edge Flight Test, 21-26, 29-31

Simulated airline flights, 21

Supersonic Laminar Flow, 32-33, 71-75

Pumping system, 8

Purifoy, Dana, 33 n

Reukauf, Carol A., 33 n

Reynolds number, 2, 3-4, 5, 6, 7-10, 18, 27, 30-31, 34

Reynolds, Osborne, 2

Schlichting, Hermann, 4, 29, 30

Schneider, Edward T., 17 n

Schubauer, G.B., 4

Skramstad, H.K., 4

Stack, John P., 23

Steers, Louis L., 17 n

Stucky, Mark P., 33 n

Suction type

continuous, 5-6, 8, 10, 24-26, 32-33

slotted, 5-6, 8-9, 22-23, 24-26

strips, 7

Swann, Michael R., 17 n

Tetervin, Neal, 5

Tidstrom, K.P., 4

Toll, Thomas A., 13 n

Tollmien, Walter, 4, 29, 30

Trujillo, Bianca M., 17 n

Vendolski, Walter, 20

Visconti, Fioravante, 4, 5

von Doenhoff, Albert E., 4

Wagner, Richard D., 23, 26 n

Wilson, James A., 20, 23

Wind tunnels

Ames 12-Foot Tunnel, 18

Langley Low-Turbulence Pressure Tunnel, 4, 18

Wright, Howard T., 14 n

Young, Ronald, 23, 26 n

About the Author

Albert L. Braslow graduated from the Guggenheim School of Aeronautics, New York University, in 1942 (with a Bachelor of Aeronautical Engineering degree) and continued with post-graduate studies at the University of Virginia, UCLA, George Washington University. and Langley Research Center. During over 50 years of research in fundamental and applied aircraft and space-vehicle aerodynamics at and for the Langley Research Center of the National Aeronautics and Space Administration (previously the National Advisory Committee for Aeronautics), he has published over 60 technical reports, book chapters, and encyclopedia sections. Included in his research were activities at subsonic, transonic, supersonic, and hypersonic speeds in the areas of wing design, boundary layers, stability and control, aircraft performance, propulsion aerodynamics, aerodynamic loads and heating, wind-tunnel techniques, advanced technology evaluation and integration, and development and documentation of space-vehicle design criteria for structures. As an internationally-known pioneering researcher on laminar-flow control and transition from laminar to turbulent flow, he has lectured on these disciplines for the American Institute of Aeronautics and Astronautics, the [North Atlantic Treaty Organization's] Advisory Group for Aeronautical Research and Development, the University of Texas (Austin), George Washington University, University of Tennessee Space Institute, University of Virginia, University of California (Davis), the Continuing Education Program of the University of Kansas for eight years, and the Lewis and Ames Research Centers of NASA.

Monographs in Aerospace History

This is the thirteenth publication in a new series of special studies prepared under the auspices of the NASA History Program. The **Monographs in Aerospace History** series is designed to provide a wide variety of investigations relative to the history of aeronautics and space. These publications are intended to be tightly focused in terms of subject, relatively short in length, and reproduced in inexpensive format to allow timely and broad dissemination to researchers in aerospace history. Suggestions for additional publications in the **Monographs in Aerospace History** series are welcome and should be sent to Roger D. Launius, Chief Historian, Code ZH, National Aeronautics and Space Administration, Washington, DC, 20546. Previous publications in this series are:

Launius, Roger D. and Gillette, Aaron K. Compilers. *Toward a History of the Space Shuttle: An Annotated Bibliography*. (Monographs in Aerospace History, Number 1, 1992)

Launius, Roger D. and Hunley, J. D. Compilers. *An Annotated Bibliography of the Apollo Program*. (Monographs in Aerospace History, Number 2, 1994)

Launius, Roger D. *Apollo: A Retrospective Analysis*. (Monographs in Aerospace History, Number 3, 1994)

Hansen, James R. *Enchanted Rendezvous: John C. Houbolt and the Genesis of the Lunar-Orbit Rendezvous Concept*. (Monographs in Aerospace History, Number 4, 1995)

Gorn, Michael H. *Hugh L. Dryden's Career in Aviation and Space*. (Monographs in Aerospace History, No. 5, 1996).

Powers, Sheryll Goecke. *Women in Aeronautical Engineering at the Dryden Flight Research Center, 1946-1994*. (Monographs in Aerospace History, No. 6, 1997).

Portree, David S.F. and Trevino, Robert C. Compilers. *Walking to Olympus: A Chronology of Extravehicular Activity (EVA)*. (Monographs in Aerospace History, No. 7, 1997).

Logsdon, John M. Moderator. *The Legislative Origins of the National Aeronautics and Space Act of 1958: Proceedings of an Oral History Workshop.* (Monographs in Aerospace History, No. 8, 1998).

Rumerman, Judy A. Compiler. *U.S. Human Spaceflights: A Record of Achievement, 1961-1998.* (Monographs in Aerospace History, No. 9, 1998).

Portree, David S.F. *NASA's Origins and the Dawn of the Space Age.* (Monographs in Aerospace History, No. 10, 1998).

Logsdon, John M. *Together in Orbit: The Origins of International Cooperation in the Space Station Program.* (Monographs in Aerospace History, No. 11, 1998).

Phillips, W. Hewitt. *Journey in Aeronautical Research: A Career at NASA Langley Research Center.* (Monographs in Aerospace History, No. 12, 1998).

www.ingramcontent.com/pod-product-compliance
Lightning Source LLC
Chambersburg PA
CBHW081237090426
42738CB00016B/3334